Change Me

The Ultimate Life-Change Handbook

Rick Thomas

The Counseling Solutions Group, Inc.

Copyright

Change Me - The Ultimate Life-Change Handbook

ISBN: 978-1-7323854-0-5

LCCN: 2018906249

Cover Artwork by: Elieser Loewenthal

Edited by: Sarah Hayhurst

© 2018 by Rick Thomas

Published by The Counseling Solutions Group, Inc.

120 Goodridge Court

Greer, SC 29651

RickThomas.Net

Dedication

To Lucia, Tristen, Haydn, and Ansa

Table of Contents

Introduction   7

Make the Most of It   9

First Unique Step   17

Perfect Self-Help Book   25

Five Things to Know   33

Only Four Problems In Life   41

Twelve Universal Assumptions   49

Why Do I Do That?   57

When I Kept Silent   67

Two Essentials to Change   75

The Control of Others   83

Taking Thoughts Captive   93

God Puts You to Death   103

Beyond Your Ability?   111

Overcoming Self-Reliance   121

Four Steps to Change   129

You Must Know These   137

Five Marks of Change   147

Pre-Forgiveness Comes First   155

Hardest Way to Help Someone   163

Powerful Way to Help Someone   171

Being Intentionally Intrusive   181

An Unchangeable Situation   189

Most Perfect Relationship   197

Leading Your Wife in Conversations   205

Build and Enjoy Community Life   215

Reason to Marry or Reconcile   225

How to Kill Your Marriage   233

What Is Your Wife Thinking?   241

Secondary Considerations   249

Orientation of Your Home   257

Are You a Restful Soul?   265

Improve Your Prayer Life   273

Stop Reading - Start Doing   281

It Is Finished   289

About the Author   291

Endorsements

"Nobody, and I mean, nobody comes close to practically applying theology to your thirsty, wounded, struggling, heartbroken, weary soul like Rick Thomas. The title is not hyperbole. This book will change your life. I know that for a fact, because it changed mine."

Todd Friel, Wretched TV and Radio

"In recent history, the battle of who has the authority over the human psyche/soul has intensified. We now live in a day and age where someone we hardly know—usually possessing an advanced degree and often having a fancy office—is permitted to instruct us on how to live our lives and how to understand our souls. We are regularly told that the most educated—who have accepted popular ideas—are best positioned to authoritatively help us make positive-lasting life changes. But God still insists in His Word that it is His wisdom—gained through an intimate covenant relationship with Himself and transparently shared with His people—which enables positive change, and that is precisely what Rick Thomas emphasizes in his book, *Change Me - The Ultimate Life-Change Handbook*

This book is not a self-help guide, a life-enrichment ploy, or the newest fad in life-coaching paradigms and humanistic solutions cloaked in Christian verbiage. Rather, from the outset, Rick makes it clear that it is the Holy Spirit who alone can produce lasting life changes. What is also powerfully expressed throughout the book is Rick's testimony of how God's grace has changed his life.

Rick emphasizes God's sovereignty and the necessity of faith/dependence, he offers wide perspectives where it is helpful to understand God's grand kingdom plan, and he gets down to the "nitty gritty" when necessary and beneficial. What is most helpful in reading through this book is the practical application of Scripture with which readers will be able to personally identify and implement into their own lives. I highly recommend Rick Thomas' book for personal or group studies."

Dr. Daniel R. Berger II, author, speaker, & Director of Alethia International Ministries

"Rick's writing is rich in grace and wisdom and solidly founded on God's Word. His words and ministry have been used to influence and change my life and the lives of those around me. I am grateful for this book and recommend it to all Christians of every age. Take his advice and read through it with your family, or a close friend. I'm sure you'll be delightfully surprised and edified with the conversation that will follow."

Lisa Rice, Wife and Mother

"Rick's goal is to point you toward Christ. His writing leaves me feeling encouraged and at peace while bringing to light areas in my life that obviously need work, though until after reading his books were not so obvious to me. There are very few people like Rick who can bring up a problem in your life, show you the solution (pointing you toward a Christ-centered life, in a kind and loving way), and leave you feeling encouraged and energized."

Hudson Cole, University Student

"If you are looking for help in your Christian walk, or if you are helping a friend in theirs, Rick's books and ministry provide the best practical help to live out the gospel while not minimizing soul care. This book is perfect for small group discussions, or for use in one-on-one counseling situations.

4

Ultimately, it can change one's character by connecting the gospel to your daily life."

Mark Grant, Biblical Counselor

"Rick has a unique and needed gift of making scripture applicable. God's Word must practically speak to me if I am to be conformed to the image of His Son. I find Rick's writing easy to read and understand, yet somehow his soft, gentle approach cuts right through to my heart. This book lives up to its name. It will change you. It will bless you."

Julie Hansen, Wife and Mother

"Rick Thomas is an excellent author. His writing is one of a kind. He understands a lot of issues that people face today, and he gives biblical and practical counsel on a variety of topics! He is also very gospel-centered in all his books. As a graduate of his program, I highly recommend his website and resources!"

- Dr. R. Douglas Graham, Pastor and Biblical Counselor

Introduction

Change Me - The Ultimate Life-Change Handbook will change your life if you let it. It will also improve your relationships—marriage, parenting, small group, the local church, and other community contexts where you are connecting with people. I wrote these chapters with practicality in view. At the end of each chapter is a call to action (CTA) opportunity that will challenge you to do something with what you read.

It is best to read this book with someone you can talk to about the content. If you're married, your spouse is the perfect candidate. Perhaps your small group is looking for solid, practical, sanctification content. You have found it. Share this book with your friend. I've divided the chapters into eleven categories:

1. Making the Most of the Journey – Chapters 1 to 2
2. Your Self-Help Book – Chapters 3 to 4
3. Discipleship Worldview – Chapters 5 to 6
4. Personal Struggles – Chapters 7 to 14
5. The Change Process – Chapters 15 to 17
6. Helping People Change – Chapters 18 to 22
7. Communication – Chapters 23 to 25
8. Marriage and Family – Chapters 26 to 30
9. Work to Rest – Chapter 31
10. A Praying Life – Chapter 32
11. Time to Apply – Chapter 33 to 34

Perhaps you're looking for something on communication. You can skip the first six categories and read the three chapters on communication. Maybe you want to get into the heart of your marriage struggles. Great. You can start with section eight. There are five chapters for you to read.

The most effective way to read this book is to understand the whole process of change; thus, starting with the first chapter, "Making the Most of the Journey," is the best place to begin. The chapters are set up logically with one building upon the next one. Regardless of where you jump into this book, the key to your transformation will be how often you use the book. Reading it once and moving on to the next thing is not the intended purpose of this book. It will take you years to master this material.

Restatement: it will take years for you "to be mastered" by this material. Read it often. Grab a nugget. Let that be your meditation for the day. Share your daily thoughts with a friend. Talk about it. Practice what you read daily. Teach someone what you learned. The teacher always learns more than the student. If you can teach others what you are actively practicing in your relationships, you will be the master of and mastered by this resource. Let this life-transforming journey begin today.

Rick
Greenville, South Carolina
2018

Chapter 1

Make the Most of It

Most people look for resources like this because they want something to change in their lives or relationships. Perhaps their marriage is in trouble. Maybe a parent is struggling with a child. Sometimes life can take unexpected turns. All of us have found ourselves in those places. When trouble comes into our lives, people look for answers. They are looking for help, and a Christian perspective on how to change is a reliable option for some of our most difficult challenges.

The Lord has been merciful to His church by giving us better ways and means to respond to the problems in our lives. A better way is what this book offers. As with all things, there are limits, and this book is no exception. The method of bringing help to people is not always satisfying in the sense that it will give you exactly what you want the way you want it, every time.

Without a clear understanding of what you're about to do, you may be disappointed with the process, as well as the results you hope to enjoy. *Change Me* may be a refreshing drink of water. It may guide you, but it won't change you.

Thinking any book can do that is shortsighted. It is one of the most common misunderstandings about life change books, which makes one wonder why they are so popular. We read them like chain smoking, but they do not change us. If your heart's desire is to change, I want to give you six things to consider before you embark on what I hope is a transformative journey. Without knowing these essential elements about life change, you may be disappointed about your experience and possibly miss what the Lord could be writing into your life (Genesis 50:20).

Count the Cost

"For which of you, desiring to build a tower, does not first sit down and count the cost, whether he has enough to complete it?" (Luke 14:28).

Before Jesus said these words to the crowd that was following Him, He told them if they did not die, they could not be His disciples (Luke 14:27). Before He said that, He told them they must hate their fathers, mothers, brothers, sisters, and even hate their lives if they wanted to follow Him (Luke 14:26). Nothing has changed since that time.

We continue to play the game by His rules. Are you ready to die? Are you willing to die to all your dreams, hopes, and aspirations? Death to self is not my idea. Those are the words of Jesus. He did not come to earth to find and enjoy the best marriage, the greatest children, or the most money. Quite the contrary. He came to die, and the only way you can find what you are looking for, which is peace with God, yourself, and others, is through the same death portal.

Assess yourself: Are you ready to die to yourself? Do you know what that means?

Change Is Not the Only Option

"So to keep me from becoming conceited because of the surpassing greatness of the revelations, a thorn was given me in the flesh, a messenger of Satan to harass me, to keep me from becoming conceited" (2 Corinthians 12:7).

Too often people buy books for the wrong reasons. Most of the time the reason is simple: "I want my situation to change." They do not count the cost, and they are not aware of the costs. It was the will of the Lord to kill His Son

(Isaiah 53:10), and it was the will of the Lord to give Paul a depressing thorn in his flesh, one that He never removed from the great apostle even though Paul wanted it removed. The Lord pondered his request and decided to give him something else.

I shared some of these ideas with a nominal Christian lady a few years ago, and she said, "I don't care about that kind of suffering. I just want my husband to be kind to me." She never changed her position, and neither did her marriage change. Sometimes the way the Lord brings change into our lives is not how we want it, but if you want this book to work for you, you must be open to all of the options, not just the options you prefer. It is possible you will not get what you want the way you want it.

Assess yourself: Are you okay with praying, "Not my will but your will be done?"

Focus on Yourself

"Why do you see the speck that is in your brother's eye, but do not notice the log that is in your own eye? Or how can you say to your brother, 'Let me take the speck out of your eye,' when there is the log in your own eye? You hypocrite, first take the log out of your own eye, and then you will see clearly to take the speck out of your brother's eye" (Matthew 7:3–5).

The easiest trap for a person to fall into during relational conflict is to talk about what is wrong with the other person—whether it is a spouse, child, parent, or friend. Will you embrace the following as your own?

I will not say anything critical about anyone else. I will focus on myself and what I need to change, rather than on what someone else needs to change. If I have something negative to say about someone else, I will frame it in the

11

most positive light while expecting myself to adapt, rather than demanding that they are the ones who must change for me to be happy.

This book can be effective if you will own what you just read. You do not go to a fitness center because someone else is obese. You go to change you. If you do not see your problems as opportunities for you to change, this book will not work for you. Make this your truth: What I have done to Christ is far worse than what any person has done to me. This God-centered, gospel-motivated idea must stabilize your heart while focusing your mind during this season of your life. To miss this point is to lose the advantage of having the Lord working in your life.

Assess yourself: Do you understand how the log that Jesus talked about is more important for you to address than the speck in the other person's eye?

Guard Your Heart

"Brothers, if anyone is caught in any transgression, you who are spiritual should restore him in a spirit of gentleness. Keep watch on yourself, lest you too be tempted. Bear one another's burdens, and so fulfill the law of Christ" (Galatians 6:1–2).

Are you the caught person or the restorer in Paul's verse? It is a trick question. You are both. You, like me, are caught in many sins. We have several things that have been historically and habitually wrong in our lives. And we should be restorers. We should be actively engaging our friends and family, trying to help them change. If you are coming to this point in your life because you hope the other person will change, that is fine, but there are requirements on you to help restore them.

You must assist them to change through a spirit of gentleness. You must keep watch on yourself, or you will sin mightily against them. Are you a gentle restorer of others? Do you sin against them because they are not changing according to your expectations and timetable? If you fail as a restorer of others, you are interfering with and circumventing what the Lord could be doing in their lives. Sinning in response to sin is never the right answer. Guard your heart. If you are reading this book because of a broken relationship, how you think about and respond to the other person could be the thing that makes this book a success or a failure.

Assess yourself: Are you a gentle restorer?

You Cannot Change Anyone

"And the Lord's servant must not be quarrelsome but kind to everyone, able to teach, patiently enduring evil, correcting his opponents with gentleness. God may perhaps grant them repentance leading to a knowledge of the truth" (2 Timothy 2:24–25).

On your best day, you are a waterer and a planter (1 Corinthians 3:6). You cannot change anyone. Only the Lord can bring change, and it is not a guarantee that He will do what you want Him to do when you want Him to do it. The time you spend in this book is your season to change. You may have a spouse, child, or friend that you want to see change. That is your thought for them. It is your idea. It is your hope. It is not a wrong hope, but it is yours. It might not be the Lord's will to change them now or at all.

You must adjust your heart accordingly. The mind of the Lord on these matters is not yours to understand entirely (Deuteronomy 29:29). His ways are far superior (Isaiah 55:8–9). The question for you is whether you will be okay if you do not receive the change that you hope for as you go through this process. There is grace for unexpected and undesired outcomes to your circumstances.

Assess yourself: Will you be okay if the Lord chooses not to bring the change you hope would happen in your life?

Expect to Be Surprised

"Lazarus has died, and for your sake I am glad that I was not there, so that you may believe" (John 11:14–15).

I lost one wife and two children through an adulterous affair. I lost two brothers through murder. I lost a dad to drunkenness. I say this to say that you may not get what you want. But there is one thing I know: the Lord is good. God's goodness is not pie-in-the-sky dreaming or bumper-sticker theology. It is a truth branded on the hearts of all those who have experienced God in the crucible of suffering (John 12:24; Daniel 3:25).

The wisdom of God is wiser than us, and His weakness is stronger than us (1 Corinthians 1:18–25). We can sing about our great and powerful God, but the real question is whether you are willing to take the death march to the crucible. Your suffering may be the perfect thing for you. To change it, though it seems reasonable, might be the worst thing for you. The child who gets everything he wants is not the better for it. The child who finds peace through the disappointments of life has found the secret to living well in God's world (Philippians 4:11–13).

Assess yourself: Will you ask the Father to do His will in your life and make you okay with His will even if you do not get what you want?

Call to Action

The hardest and most challenging advice you may receive could be practically embracing the ideas put forth in this chapter. If you can do this, your journey to change can be profitable, and the aftermath can be rewarding—regardless of how your circumstances unfold for you.

If you are looking for a life change, one of the best things you can do is answer the assessment questions provided at the end of the six headings. After you finish those questions, I have a few more that will prepare you for the journey.

1. Count the Cost – What does it mean for you to die to your dreams, hopes, and aspirations? Are you willing to give up all of them, plus your life, to follow Christ?

2. Change Is Not the Only Option – What if the Lord does not want to change your situation according to your expectations? How could this kind of thorn be God's strength in your weakness and a blessing to others?

3. Focus on Yourself – Are you more apt to focus on another person's need to change or on how you need to change? Are you able to live in the peace that God offers even when others are not changing? Why or why not?

4. Guard Your Heart – Are you a gentle restorer of others? Are you tempted to sin when you think about how they are "caught" in something? How do you need to change?

5. You Cannot Change Anyone – Will you accept God's timing on improving your situation? Will you accept the possibility that He may never change your situation? How did you answer these two questions, and why did you respond the way you did?

6. Expect to Be Surprised – The death of Christ was hard news for the disciples to receive. In fact, they left Him; they denied knowing Him. What if the Lord allows something to happen that does not make sense to you? What if His ways are radically different from your ways?

Prayerfully consider the questions in this chapter. You do not have to move on right now. Perhaps it would be better to share this content with a friend and you both talk about it. The primary goal is not to read this book to complete it. Your main goal is for God to change you. Take your time. Pace yourself. Reflect deeply. Pray often. Ask the Father to help you change what He's pressing on your heart now. When you're ready, you can go to the next chapter.

Chapter 2

First Unique Step

Can you help me with [what I'm going through]? I'm struggling, and I want my [problems] to end. Will you advise me? How can I work through [this]? Will this [situation] ever go away? Problems come and go as sparks from fire flies upward. Trouble and trials began with the fall of humanity, and they will not go away until Christ comes to rescue us.

Working through pain is part of the human experience, but it does not have to defeat you (2 Corinthians 4:7–10). Whether you're talking about your problems or another person's problems, there is one truth on which you can hang your hat: God's grace is sufficient (2 Corinthians 12:10).

God's grace is broader and deeper than your problems, which is why, when working through problems, your starting point must begin from this Christian worldview. I realize God's all-sufficient grace sounds too simplistic, but that does not matter. What you think about truth is not what makes truth true. God's Word is true. Period. It does not require your intellectual ascent to make it so.

There is no unfixable problem outside of God's empowering grace, though God's favor does not mean a resolution to your problems will be according to your timetable or expectations. It does mean there is grace for whatever the sovereign Lord is writing into your life narrative.

In the Beginning

When you begin addressing your problems, you have to start at the right place. Your beginning will not only define your journey, but it will determine how you finish. Your beginning is your presupposition.

That is your starting point. Everything that follows flows out of and is affected by your presuppositional worldview. For the Christian, the starting point is always God. He is the beginning. He is the window through which we think about life, especially our problems.

A person's belief system is the foundation for which he or she works at problem-solving. It is not tenable for a Christian to attempt solving his or her problems while detached from a theologically precise understanding of God.

1. Is God your starting point?
2. Is He the window through which you see, discern, and solve your problems?

Let's assume you are a Christian, and you have a Christo-centric, faith-based worldview. If so, you are set up for the best possible outcome. You can be fully confident that you will be okay regardless of the twists and turns you may experience (Philippians 1:6).

There is unmerited favor for the outcome, and you can rest in God's sovereign scripting. This kind of God-centered presupposition brings rest even in a storm. It releases you from trying to force or manipulate an outcome according to how you want things to be.

"There is a way that seems right to a man, but its end is the way to death" (Proverbs 14:12).

"For my thoughts are not your thoughts, neither are your ways my ways, declares the LORD" (Isaiah 55:8).

You do not want a yes to your prayers if the Lord is saying no. You want what God wants even if His ways bring a bumpier than expected path (1 Corinthians 1:25; 2 Corinthians 1:8–9).

"For the sake of Christ, then, I am content with weaknesses, insults, hardships, persecutions, and calamities. For when I am weak, then I am strong" (2 Corinthians 12:10).

The reason a Christian thinks this way is because he or she is assured personal peace through present trials, plus an ending that is beyond anything his finite mind could imagine. (See Ephesians 3:2–21; Philippians 4:6–7.) Your faith does not mean you should blindly accept everything that comes into your life without biblical analysis. It also does not say, when circumstances lead you down a path that is not according to your liking, that you should resign yourself to fatalism.

Personal problems are not a call to lie down, give up, or turn inward as though there is nothing you can do about them or should do about them. God allows problems in your life for many reasons. A problem is your call to trust God while working out the redemption He is working in you (Philippians 2:12–13).

Problem-solving is your opportunity to discern God, know God, and mature in God while seeking to understand what He has in store for you. And because you are working above the net of God's grace, you can confidently move forward knowing that all will be well with your soul.

Start Here

How do you approach your problems? Do you begin problem-solving knowing everything will be okay? Can we be honest? I think most of us start our problem-solving task with the desired end in mind, and if we can accomplish that end, we will be okay. That mindset starts this way:

1. We experience something undesirable, and we want it to change.
2. Before we look to God, we look for a quick exit from our problems.

3. Even when we look to God, it is more about a plea for Him to change our circumstances.

"But he is unchangeable, and who can turn him back? What he desires, that he does. For he will complete what he appoints for me, and many such things are in his mind" (Job 23:13–14).

If your strategy is like what I have described, it's time to rethink your problem-solving strategies. If your primary goal is to change your circumstances, you may set yourself up for ongoing suffering and continued relational dysfunction. I am not saying you should not pray for changes in your circumstances (Matthew 26:39; 2 Corinthians 12:8). Who knows? It may be God's will to change things to how you want them.

But if not (Luke 22:42; Daniel 3:17–18) . . .

Yes, pray. By all means, ask the Father to change things for you. That is an excellent prayer because God can do the impossible (Luke 18:27). If He wills, He can do this, or He can do that. (See James 4:15.) The problem is when you try to steer God's hands toward an outcome you think is right. James called this arrogance, which He categorized as sin. If you are tempted to guide God's hands, you must change.

"Instead you ought to say, 'If the Lord wills, we will live and do this or that,' As it is, you boast in your arrogance. All such boasting is evil. So whoever knows the right thing to do and fails to do it, for him it is sin" (James 4:15–17).

God Uses Sin Sinlessly

The Lord is the only person who is wise enough, strong enough, and holy enough to permit suffering in your life for the sole purpose of a favorable outcome. What you think is exclusively for evil can be turned on its head and used for your good, His fame, and the benefit of millions.

"As for you, you meant evil against me, but God meant it for good, to bring it about that many people should be kept alive, as they are today" (Genesis 50:20).

Not knowing God's full mind on a matter is why it is dangerous and unwise to begin your problem-solving efforts without a God-centered presupposition. Who knows, maybe the Lord has brought you into a suffering-filled season for the express purpose of doing things in your life and relationships that could only happen through suffering.

"Who knows whether you have not come to the kingdom for such a time as this?" (Esther 4:14b).

It should cause you to wonder how often you have pushed against the purposes of the Lord, as you tried to truncate His work in your life because you did not like what He was doing. The answer to Mordecai's question is, "God brought Esther into the kingdom to spread the Lord's fame." The Lord raised her up for the express purpose of putting His name and His people on display throughout the known world.

He allowed sin and suffering to accomplish His good purposes. Mordecai had the right worldview. His starting point determined how he worked the problem, as well as how things ended, and all of those things worked together for good (Romans 8:28). It is not wise to read the Bible in a detached way. The stories of Joseph and Esther make sense, and you nod in affirmation to the goodness of God through their trials.

Then the trials happen to you.

When suffering comes to your door, your theology can fall flat as your mind begins to stray from God-centered purposes. The truth taught in Sunday school loses the momentum that should sustain you, especially when Joseph's and Esther's problems become your problems. Esther and Joseph lived in the comfortable tension of gospel irony. What the world meant for evil, God meant for good because He was working His redemptive plan in the lives of His children.

Back to the Basics

The cross of Christ is the most counterintuitive event in human history. The disciples stood at the foot of that hill on that day, looking up at a dead man on a tree. He was supposed to be their leader (Mark 8:31–33). On that day, their dream died. The death of Christ threw them for a loop. There was a season when it appeared they would never recover from their disappointment. Peter denied ever knowing Him and the whole gang went spiraling into dysfunction (John 18:27).

Nothing will try your faith more than when you want something so bad, but you're unable to attain it. Unfulfilled requests are what makes the gospel so profound. It is also what makes preaching the gospel to yourself every day so necessary. Peter and his team had to go back to the basics. They needed a gospel realignment. With a shattered faith, they needed serious downtime with God to have their hearts reoriented to His truth rather than by their dreams.

"And behold, I am sending the promise of my Father upon you. But stay in the city until you are clothed with power from on high" (Luke 24:49).

They were of no value to God or their constituency because the gospel they claimed to believe was not the animating center of their lives. They were unbelieving believers—Christians who believed God, which punched their ticket to heaven, but their belief did not give them what they needed to live well on earth.

Perhaps this is you. If you are stuck in a funk and cannot seem to make any headway out of the funk, let me appeal to you to spend less time trying to get out of your funk and more time realigning your heart to the Lord. You may never fully understand what He is up to in your life. Your faith is buoyed by who God is, not by having all the answers to your problems.

Time to Stand Up

Maybe God does not want to change your circumstances. Think Joseph. Think Esther. Think Jesus. Think Paul. Reflect on any person in the Bible who did not get what they wanted. If the main thrust of your mental energy is about changing your circumstances, you are making a huge mistake.

Maybe God wants to change your circumstances. I do not know. I do know that He wants to change your heart. And if He changes your heart, your circumstances will have less control over you. The end game is not your best life now but is finding shalom with God, even when life does not make sense.

That is what Peter and his team had to do. They had to reconcile the fact that they were not going to get what they wanted, when they wanted it, and how they wanted it. Jesus was not going to be their king—not at that time. They had to become okay with their unchangeable circumstance.

Once they reconciled that in their hearts, they turned their problems and their world on its head (Acts 17:6). It is possible that what you perceive to be right is wrong. Eventually, Peter discerned this possibility, and afterward, life became less about what he wanted and more about what God wanted.

"But Peter, standing with the eleven, lifted up his voice and addressed them, 'Men of Judea and all who dwell in Jerusalem, let this be known to you, and give ear to my words'" (Acts 2:14).

One of the most powerful verses in the Bible, when considering the context of the dire situation, is Acts 2:14. There are times when a passage jumps out at you. I remember many years ago when this passage jumped out at me. It begins by saying, "But Peter, standing . . ." When you put this passage in context with the most recent events in Peter's life, it is staggering. One of the last times we saw Peter, he was not standing or defending the faith.

He was cursing and denying the faith. But then something transformative happened to this man. He did not get what he wanted. He got something far better. It was so much better that he went from denying the Lord to proclaiming the goodness of the Lord. Praising God is my hope for you. Your life or circumstance may never change. I don't know. What I do know is your desired outcome cannot be your starting point. When Peter's ambitions became his point of departure, he denied the Lord.

When he exchanged his desires for the will of God, he got something transcendent. Problem-solving begins with the Lord, not with what you want. If what you want is colliding with what the Lord is giving to you, this is your first problem to solve.

Call to Action

1. Do you believe your problems are greater than God's grace? Why did you answer that way?

2. Name three bad things in your life that the Lord used for your good and His glory?

3. Are you struggling now? If so, have you surrendered the outcome to the Lord, or are you still trying to control the outcome?

Chapter 3

Perfect Self-Help Book

In the last chapter, I talked about your nonnegotiable presupposition. It is God. He is your starting point. He is the window through which you view everything in your life, assuming you are a Christian. You will never have a more solid foundation, starting point, or worldview than the Lord. He is the only person who can equip you for living well in His world.

But knowing there is a God and that He is your foundation are not enough. You must have a system of thought, a way to think like He thinks (Isaiah 55:8–9). You cannot imitate Him if you do not know what He is thinking (Ephesians 5:1). Believing in Him or His existence is not enough. You need to be fortified by Him when trouble comes (James 2:19).

"Sanctify them in the truth; your word is truth" (John 17:17).

"Finally, brothers, whatever is true, whatever is honorable, whatever is just, whatever is pure, whatever is lovely, whatever is commendable, if there is any excellence, if there is anything worthy of praise, think about these things" (Philippians 4:8)

You need a way of thinking about the human condition. To be more specific, you need a way of thinking about you. There has to be a body of knowledge that can guide you into God's truth (Philippians 4:8). If you possess this body of knowledge, you are ready to answer and engage some of your most life-perplexing questions. For example,

1. Why do you do what you do?
2. Why do you respond to life's trials the way you do?

3. Why do you affect people the way you do?

4. Why are you affected by people the way you are?

Competing Worldviews

The system of thought I am describing is called psychology. Psychology is the most accurate way to think about the human condition. It is a Bible-implied word. Just like theology is a Bible-implied word that describes what we know about God, psychology explains what we know about people.

The word psychology is a compound word that means psyche and logos. The word psyche means soul, and the word logos means the word concerning or the study of the soul. Some people say the word psyche means mind. That is part of what it means.

Whether you are talking about the mind or the soul, the meaning is the same in that you are talking about your inner being. Humans consist of two parts: nonorganic or spiritual and organic or physical. The word psychology points to the nonorganic part of a person, their inner being. For example, anthropology is the study of their outer being.

- Theology is the study of God.
- Anthropology (Anthropos Logos) is the study of people.
- Psychology is the study of our inner being.

The problem happens when different people groups compete for who knows best about the inner workings of a human being. This confusion does not make psychology a bad word. It makes how we think about psychology problematic. The Christian is in the best position to think correctly about psychology because the Christian's starting point is God.

The problem is when nonbiblical or sub-biblical people groups try to foist their presuppositions and worldviews onto the word psychology. When they do this, psychology becomes twisted and unhelpful. This would be similar to an anthropologist studying bones and making a case for evolution. Reasoning is circular: an evolutionistic presupposition is going to lead to an evolutionistic conclusion, which will affirm an evolutionistic presupposition.

I expect the non-Christian anthropologist to study bones and tell me why evolution is true. Before I became a believer, I bought into many of those conclusions. After I had become a believer, my presupposition changed, which changed my conclusions about the study of humanity. The same applies to the field of psychology. The non-Christian person is entitled to his opinions, and I am entitled to mine, which is why I reject his presupposition, his worldview, and his conclusions. (Of course, he rejects mine, too.)

If there is anything he or she says that I accept, it is because I filtered it through my God-centered presupposition. From my worldview, it can only be true if it lines up with God's Word. The Canon (God's Word) becomes the rule from which I determine what is true and false.

The Author of the Psyche

In Genesis 2:7 we learn that God breathed into Adam and he became animated—he became a living soul. The Lord was the author and creator of the nonorganic (psychology) and the organic parts (anthropology) of humanity. God made Adam's psyche. His soul did not come through random evolutionary processes. It came by the predetermined wisdom and action of God. The Lord thought of the soul. He created the soul. He was the architect of the soul.

"For by him all things were created, in heaven and on earth, visible and invisible, whether thrones or dominions or rulers or authorities—all things were created through him and for him" (Colossians 1:16).

This is a big deal, and it is a faith issue, which is the same for everyone. We all believe what we believe by faith. I am a Christian. Therefore, my system of thought is uniquely God-centered. That is my faith.

27

The Author of the Logos

Paul, under the controlling, illuminating, and inspiring power of God, gives us insight into how our Bible came to us. He tells us in 2 Timothy 3:16 that the Lord breathed again. This time, He breathed into selected men, whom He chose to write words. This divine exercise inspired the writers of the Bible. In time, those words breathed out by God were put into one edition. The culmination of this process gave us the Bible.

"His divine power has granted to us all things that pertain to life and godliness, through the knowledge of him who called us to his own glory and excellence" (2 Peter 1:3).

The Bible is a book that tells us about God, humanity, and life. Everything we know about God (theology) comes from the Bible. No other book in the world gives us new or undiscovered information about God. Any other author from any other book that tells us about God (theology) gained his or her insight from the Bible. All books about God are supported or discredited by the clear teaching of God's Word.

The same goes for psychology. The Lord created the soul (psyche), and He created the logos (Word) concerning the psyche. The purest soul book ever written is God's Word. Any literature outside of God's Word that seeks to explain our souls (psyche) is supported or discredited by the clear teaching of God's Word.

It is not wrong for someone to write about the soul. But the litmus test that verifies an author's truth claims about the soul is God's psychology book.

Thus, you can conclude the following:

1. God created the soul.
2. God created the soul book.

3. God gave us psychology: the Word concerning the soul or the study of the soul.

My Psychologist Is Greater

The greatest soul (psyche) care provider who ever lived was Jesus Christ. As Son of God, He created the soul (psyche), and He gave us the Word concerning the soul (logos).) John spoke of Jesus and His ability as a psychologist in this way:

"Jesus on his part did not entrust himself to them, because he knew all people and needed no one to bear witness about man, for he himself knew what was in man" (John 2:24–25).

Imagine sitting on the Savior's couch, being analyzed by Him. He would be able to figure you out quickly and tell you exactly what is wrong with you and what you need to do.

Jesus was a Master Psychologist because He studied the soul book (Luke 2:52). Any person who spends their life studying the soul book can grow in their understanding and practice of the purest psychology known to humanity.

The Christian has a distinct advantage over any non-Christian when it comes to the study of the soul (psychology) because he has God's inspired Word—the psychology book. Non-Christians grope in the dark when it comes to understanding psychology because the Bible is a mystery to them, if not downright foolish (Deuteronomy 29:29; 1 Corinthians 1:18–25, 2:14).

The Christian has the illuminating power of the Spirit of God to guide him into all the truth contained in the Word of God (John 16:13, 17:17). The Christian also has the providential guidance of a sovereign Lord, who orchestrates life events on behalf of His children (Genesis 50:20).

Additionally, the Christian has a community of psychologists (God's children), who are always pursuing a better understanding of the psychology book while seeking to make practical applications for God's glory and each other's mutual benefit (Hebrews 10:24–25).

Thus, you can conclude the following:

1. You have the Word to guide you.

2. You have the Spirit to guide you.

3. You have your illuminated self to guide you.

4. You have the community of faith to guide you.

Competing Bibles

Problems arise and skirmishes ensue when people deviate from the clear teaching of God's Word. Even with all the aforementioned protective measures that we have, it is still easy to drift from pure psychology—the study of the soul. I will not elaborate on all the ways in which our psychology runs afoul, but I will mention the most common one I encounter: God's psychology book versus the world's psychology book.

We call our psychology book the Bible. They [secular psychologists] call their psychology book the DSM-V, (It used to be DSM-I, II, III, and IV.) Their bible has gone through five iterations. We are still working with our first one, including the Old and New Testaments. The DSM-V has its language, which is often communicated through acronyms: OCD, ADD, ADHD, and so forth. The secular psychologist also uses disorder language, meaning most of the problems they describe are disorders. Let me illustrate.

Alex does not behave well at school. He misbehaves. His parents take him to a psychologist. The psychologist looks at Alex. He asks Alex a battery of questions, and then he questions the parents. He gives Alex a test to take.

The psychologist concludes that Alex has ADD and sets an appointment with a psychiatrist. The parents take Alex to a psychiatric appointment where the psychiatrist prescribes medication. Alex's behavior changes for the better. The conclusion is Alex has ADD.

The diagnosis begins to fall flat when you start asking better questions. What you would learn is that it does not matter to the parents what the psychologist says as long as he can fix their child. Here are a few questions I would ask his parents in a logical order.

1. Do you like Alex's new behaviors? Yes.

2. Why did he change? It was the medication.

3. How did you know he had a medical problem? We took him to a psychologist.

4. What did the psychologist say? He said Alex had ADD.

5. How did the psychologist come to that conclusion? He asked a few questions. (Subjective, nonscientific diagnosis.)

6. What was the filter he used to interpret the answers you gave him? The DSM-V.

7. How did the DSM-V come to these conclusions? I do not know.

From here it becomes convoluted. It does not matter to the parents how the psychologist came to his conclusions. They are not going to challenge his presuppositions because they like the result: Alex is better behaved, which is pragmatism that divorces itself from God's Word and possibly from all the Lord would like to do in their lives.

A Leap of Faith

The tension I have with this kind of reasoning, process, and outcome is that so many of our brothers and sisters have naively bought into the persuasive lies of our secular psychologized culture. They have willingly swallowed subjective analysis without question, which is befuddling and disheartening.

Every week I am told by a Christian about their disorder or how a relative has been diagnosed and labeled with an acronym. This kind of thinking is one of the biggest weaknesses in Christian sanctification. Our inability to understand and live out God's practicalized Word is doing as much harm to the Christian community as anything else that is assaulting it.

I believe in psychology as taught from the Bible. I hope to continue growing and maturing in the study of the soul because I want to be more like Jesus. Learning God's Word and practically living it out is the only way any of us can do that.

Call to Action

1. How would you describe your view of God's Word? Do you see it as the purest form of psychology ever given to humanity?

2. How would you describe your practice of God's Word in your life? (The most effective way to answer this question is by assessing your responses to the problems in your life.)

3. What do your responses to life's trials reveal about your understanding and practice of God's Word in your life? Are you an effective biblical psychologist?

Chapter 4

Five Things to Know

Kathryn did not grow up in a Christian home. It was during her first year of college when she learned of Christ's salvation. Recently she turned thirty and, though it's been eleven years since God saved her, there has been no transformation in a significant way. She has gained knowledge about the Bible, but being transformed by the Bible has been a challenge for her.

There is a disconnect between gaining knowledge and applying knowledge, which is keeping Kathryn from maturing in wisdom. A basic definition of wisdom is knowledge applied. Knowledge without application can lead to arrogance (1 Corinthians 8:1–2) while application without knowledge can lead to foolishness (Proverbs 14:1). Kathryn has knowledge, but she has not been able to apply it in ways that transform her.

I would not say she is arrogant, but she is frustrated. She wants to change, but she does not know how. And this is where the Bible excels; it teaches you how to change. It does this because that is what it was designed to do. (Read Psalm 119.)

The Bible speaks clearly to all our the problems in life (2 Peter 1:3–4) because it is the soul book. As said in the last chapter, the more technical term for the Bible is the psychology book. It is stunning that God would give us such a means of grace to help us change. Your best course of action is to pursue this divinely-inspired book heartily.

"All Scripture is breathed out by God and profitable for teaching, for reproof, for correction, and for training in righteousness, that the man of God may be complete, equipped for every good work" (2 Timothy 3:16–17).

Because of human fallenness, there is irony with the perfect psychology book: it contains God's words, but we don't change. Kathryn has not learned how to profit from the Word of God. She is stuck. The problem in view here is not the ineffectiveness of the Bible but what is going on in Kathryn's mind and life that keeps her from being mastered by the Bible.

Who would have thought the most popular book ever written, which is probably the most undervalued and mocked book ever written, has the clearest and most accurate answers to the problems of humanity.

- What do you think about the Bible?
- Do you believe the Bible is the clearest and most accurate tool you have to understand the human condition?

The implication here is that you should be doing more than reading it on a daily basis. Many people read their Bibles every day, but there is a difference between reading the Bible and being mastered by the Bible. The way to be mastered by the Bible is to know how to connect God's Word to what is inside of you. Therefore, you must know yourself (psyche) and God's Word (logos) and make the appropriate connections.

Know What Is in You

Knowing the soul is where Jesus becomes Exhibit A on how to do this. He was a Master at applying the Word of God to His life (as well as to the lives of others). You see His ability to do this in the last two verses of John, chapter two.

"But Jesus on his part did not entrust himself to them, because he knew all people and needed no one to bear witness about man, for he himself knew what was in man" (John 2:24–25).

34

Here is the context. Jesus was having a conversation with some Jews about destroying the temple and His eventual resurrection. These Jews were trying to trick Him. As the conversation was winding down in verses 18–22, John gives a commentary on the conversation Jesus was having with the Jews when he reveals why Jesus did not entrust Himself to them. John said Jesus did not entrust Himself to them because He knew what was in man.

Jesus' inside knowledge is incredible. Christ knew exactly what to say and what to do because He knew what was in man. Having this kind of inside information is your goal: to understand what is in you so that you can change. Jesus knew individuals because He understood the Bible (the soul book), and He understood how to apply the Bible to the human condition (or the soul of man) (Luke 2:42).

Become a Psychologist

You can be similar to Jesus in understanding and practice. He was a master psychologist. The art of discipleship, which is what Jesus did, is taking the Bible and applying it to humanity. Because of God's favor on your life and by the Spirit's enabling, you possess all you need (soul book) to figure out the human condition (soul) while bringing solutions to it (2 Peter 1:3–4). You are a little psychologist, so to speak.

The illuminating and empowering Spirit of God in you (1 Corinthians 2:14) never leaves you in the dark about what to do with your problems (or the problems of others). After regeneration (John 3:7), you can grow up (1 Peter 2:2) into Christlikeness (Hebrews 5:12–14). It is possible to learn how to master God's Word and be mastered by it.

Kathryn was not connecting these dots, which her inability to make appropriate application to her life demonstrated. She had been to numerous Bible studies and had been diligently reading the Bible for eleven years, but personal transformation was not happening.

Jesus and Kathryn are the same, as far as being fully human. But His ability to understand and apply the Word of God was more transformative. Knowing and applying the Bible is the difference between heaven and hell, life and death, and maturity and immaturity. This kind of understanding of God's Book is what released Jesus to speak powerfully and authoritatively into the lives of others.

The most effective Christians are those who have a rich understanding of God's Word and the ability to apply it accurately to themselves as well as to others. The Word of God and the Spirit of God gives you this extraordinary perception.

This twofold gift is why some of the things Jesus said seemed so off-the-wall. He functioned with greater insight and clarity than most of the people in His day. You see an illustration of this when He was talking to Nicodemus about being born again. His statements completely flabbergasted Nicodemus. The educated Pharisee even asked in response, "How can a man be born when he is old? Can he enter a second time into his mother's womb and be born?" (John 3:4).

Nick knew a lot about the Bible, but he did not understand the Bible the way it needed to be understood. What appeared to be odd to him was perfect psychology to Jesus because He knew what was in man: He understood Himself and others.

Know What Is in People

If you can figure out yourself and can bring biblical clarity to your life, you will not have a difficult time figuring out and helping others. Each person is cut from the same Adamic human cloth. You do not need to know seven billion different people. You do not need to know every malady known to man. You only need to know what's in you, and the Bible is the book that will accurately give you that information. The Bible is clear, concise, insightful, and essential for sorting things out.

"For the Word of God is living and active, sharper than any two-edged sword, piercing to the division of soul and of spirit, of joints and of marrow, and discerning the thoughts and intentions of the heart. And no creature is hidden from his sight, but all are naked and exposed to the eyes of him to whom we must give account" (Hebrews 4:12–13).

Nobody is beyond the scope of the Bible's insight and clarity. Nobody is opaque when viewed through an open Bible and the Spirit's light shines on the soul. The problem is never a lack of understanding when you examine life through the lens of the Word of God.

The problem always exists when we do not want to do what the Bible plainly teaches us to do. Think about yourself. Has there been a time when God gave you clarity through His Word, but you chose not to respond to it (Luke 18:23)? I have done this many times.

1. Was it a clarity problem?
2. Was it an unwillingness to change problem?

How to Be Mastered by the Word

Here are five simple things that will help you to become a master of the Word of God. If you practice these things, you will have greater insight into what is in people, especially what is in you. In time you will become mastered by the Word of God.

Be warned: it will take work, and if you're not willing to do this kind of heavy lifting, you will not change. "But solid food is for the mature, for those who have their powers of discernment trained by constant practice to distinguish good from evil" (Hebrews 5:14).

1. Pray – Before you start reading your Bible, take the time to pray. Ask God to open your eyes to what you are reading.

2. Read – Read expectantly. God will reveal things to you about yourself. Anticipate this. Look for Bible truths like a man mining for gold. Be alert. Resist reading by rote. Read because you want to, not because you have to. Job said, "I have treasured the words of his mouth more than my portion of food" (Job 23:12b).

3. Reflect – When God illuminates your mind, stop reading and start reflecting. Think about what God is showing you in light of the Word you just read.

4. Write – Take time to write down what God has shown you. When your thoughts go from a page of the Bible, to your brain, down to your hand, and onto a piece of paper (or computer), you are probably going to own it. It will be yours to keep.

5. Teach – Within twelve hours (arbitrary timeframe) tell someone what God taught you. The teacher will learn more than the student; if you can teach what He taught you, it will master you.

As you make this simple way of studying God's Word part of your regular practice, you can also add memorization to your daily habits. If the Word of God is what it says it is, what better thing can you do than put it in your brain? Do you need inspiration for memorization? Then let me ask, "Do you want to stop sinning?" Try this verse: "I have stored up your word in my heart, that I might not sin against you" (Psalm 119:11).

As mysterious as the Bible can be to some people, it is not that complicated as far as bringing soul change, but it takes work. Though you will never fully mine it or fully understand its content, you can find what you need to change. The real question becomes whether you want to put in the effort to change. If you are willing to open your life up to the probing of the Spirit of God and the Word of God, then James says there is something good for you.

"[God] gives grace to the humble. Submit yourselves therefore to God. Resist the devil, and he will flee from you. Draw near to God, and he will draw near to you. Cleanse your hands, you sinners, and purify your hearts, you double-minded" (James 4:6b–8).

Call to Action

I guarantee if you take this chapter to heart, ask God to change you through what is written here, implement these practices into your life, you will not only change, but you will learn the Bible the way it was meant to be learned and applied.

Chapter 5

Only Four Problems In Life

Biff was your typical high school senior. He couldn't wait to graduate so that he could start college. The most pressing question during his senior year was, "Where are you going to college?" One question asked different ways:

- What are you going to do with your life?
- What do you want to be after high school?
- What degree program are you going to pursue?

The real question they were asking him was, "What do you want to be after you grow up?" This life problem was an unfortunate question for Biff. Today, Biff is forty-one years old. He has been married for seventeen years, has two children, and is thinking about a career change. He has been living with an imperceptible, low-grade discontent for the past decade.

Biff is a frustrated man.

He's frustrated with God. He's frustrated with himself. He's frustrated with his wife and children, and he's frustrated with his career. He is a couch potato that mostly checked out of life. He does not know what to do and is growing more apathetic by the day. Unfortunately for Biff, he was never discipled well. He was mostly groomed to think about his career and what he wanted to do as an adult, which is why he went to college, earned his degree, and began his dream job.

It never dawned on him (or his parents) that there were more important things in Biff's future than education. Rather than helping him with those things, his parents put on a full-court press to make sure he made good grades. Biff pleased his parents; he made excellent grades. He graduated near the top of his class in high school. The best universities in America pursued him, and he graduated in the top 5 percent of his college class.

It all looked so good. It was so promising. Biff's parents could not have been more proud. But nobody saw the chink in Biff's armor. No one equipped Biff for life. Even though he was so smart, Biff was educated to fail at life.

"Therefore do not be anxious, saying, 'What shall we eat?' or 'What shall we drink?' or 'What shall we wear?' For the Gentiles seek after all these things, and your heavenly Father knows that you need them all" (Matthew 6:31–32).

His parents did a major disservice with their education-centric worldview. His eight years in high school and college were spent solving what he believed to be the most significant problem in his life: "What do I want to be when I grow up?" What he did not know, and what no one ever told him, was that the problem he was working on should have been the least of his worries.

Now he is in a strained marriage, and his family is escalating in relational dysfunction. Biff is a well-educated man, but he can't solve his growing list of problems. He's the lead tech in his engineering firm and a failure in his family. He's ready to quit, not his job, but trying to make a go of a good marriage and family.

Here is what Biff did not know.

Problem-Solving 101

Every problem you will ever have in your life can be summed up in four categories and resolved in one order. Regardless of who you are or where you live, your problems are no different from anyone else's problems. We all may have a unique fingerprint and even want to consider ourselves different, but the real truth is that we are not different. God made one man, and every other man or woman came from that one man (Romans 5:12).

We cannot be different where it matters most, or we would need over seven billion unique solutions for our problems. When it comes to who we are and what we need, we all share in what is common to all of us.

"No temptation has overtaken you that is not common to man" (1 Corinthians 10:13).

"For we do not have a high priest who is unable to sympathize with our weaknesses, but one who in every respect has been tempted as we are, yet without sin" (Hebrews 4:15).

We have one Savior, and He can relate to all of us. One man relates to every person because all people are essentially the same. When it comes to our problems, there are only four:

1. We have a theological problem—our problem with God.
2. We have a psychological problem—our problem with ourselves.
3. We have a sociological problem—our problem with others.
4. We have an ecological problem—our problem with the world in which we live.

There are two unalterable laws to remember when working through these problems.

*   Law #1 – All problems fit into one of these four categories.
*   Law #2 – You resolve all four problems the way they are listed.

The problem with Biff is that his whole life centered around problem #4. He started and stayed there: "What do I want to be when I grow up?" Or, "How do I live in God's world?"

Our Universal Theological Problem

The number one problem in life is humanity's problem with God. I don't think I have to make a case for this: we are fundamentally flawed from the inside out, and until we solve this problem with God, nothing else really matters.

"Do not marvel that I said to you, 'You must be born again'" (John 3:7).

"But seek first the kingdom of God and his righteousness, and all these things will be added to you" (Matthew 6:33).

Our only hope is for our relationship with God to be restored to Christ. Until we fix our relationship with God, we will never be able to perceive life the way we need to see it. Only God can give us the clarity we need to live well in His world. We cannot have a nonexistent or broken or cold relationship with God and expect to be able to engage life properly. It does not work that way.

The first and biggest problem that any human must begin to resolve is his (or her) problem with God. Once we are in right standing with God and are maturing in faith, we are on the right track to begin the process of understanding ourselves.

Our Universal Psychological Problem

Psyche-logos or the study of the soul is the proper definition of the word psychology. A psychologist is a person who studies the soul. He brings observations, corrections, and counsel to soul problems. The greatest human psychologist who ever lived was Jesus Christ. The most effective psychologists in the world today are Christians who understand God's Word and can bring God's Word to bear on the souls of people.

"Then the LORD God formed the man of dust from the ground and breathed into his nostrils the breath of life, and the man became a living creature" (Genesis 2:7).

"All Scripture is breathed out by God and profitable for teaching, for reproof, for correction, and for training in righteousness" (2 Timothy 3:16).

1. God created the soul.
2. God created the Word for the soul.
3. Therefore, God is the most objective source for understanding the problems of man.

Imagine this: if you did not have a right relationship with God, it would be impossible to understand yourself correctly because God opposes proud people who will not submit to Him (James 4:6). It's an unfixable conundrum:

1. Only God can give you the clarity you need.
2. You do not submit to God.
3. God opposes you.
4. You cannot receive the intel you need to understand yourself.

Biff was having soul trouble (problem #2), relational trouble (problem #3), and job trouble (problem #4), but he never connected how those problems were because of his biggest problem with God (problem #1). He figured he would be okay if he went to church, read his Bible, and did ministry. Biff expected God to bless his endeavors.

Our Universal Sociological Problem

I spent the first twenty-five years of my life thinking about what I wanted to be after I became an adult. I worked several jobs but could never find my niche in life. It did not occur to me that my growing discontent was not because of the jobs I had or did not have, but it was because of my nonexistent relationship with God.

After God had regenerated me, I began pursuing Him in earnest. Though I was not initially aware of what was happening to me, the thing that became most apparent was that the more I began to understand God, the more I began to understand myself. Studying God through the mirror of His Word (James 1:25) gave me a clearer picture of who I was and what I needed to change. The effect of this process was that the more I began to understand myself, the more I began to understand other people.

1. You cannot understand other people well without first understanding yourself.

2. You cannot understand yourself correctly without first understanding God.

That is the order, and it cannot be altered or circumvented. Biff had an average-to-stagnant relationship with God because the Lord was not the most important thing in his life (Matthew 6:21, 24). The most profound effect of his stagnated relationship with God was the impact it had on Biff. Though his parents went to great lengths to prepare him on the job front, he was horribly equipped to solve his personal problems, marriage problems, or family problems. Notice how Paul talked about this logical progression when he was talking to Timothy:

"For if someone does not know how to manage his own household, how will he care for God's church?" (1 Timothy 3:5).

Did you see the implication of Paul's progressive order for problem-solving?

1. The pastor should be solving his personal issues.

2. Then he must be able to lead his family.

3. Lastly, he should be qualified to lead the church.

Notice Paul's progression:

1. Work on the theological problem: grow in your understanding of God.
2. Work on the psychological problem: mature in Christ.
3. Work on the sociological problem: lead others.

Our Universal Ecological Problem

This last problem is where Biff began, which proved to be his demise. It is usually where most people focus. "What do you do?" is one of the most common questions a man will ask another man. It is not as common for a man to ask another man, "Talk to me about your relationship with God. What are you learning and how are you growing in Christ?" The questions we ask each other and the kinds of conversations we have reveal who we are (Luke 6:45).

I've called our last problem an "ecological" problem for the sake of rhyming, though I am stretching the word ecology. It's not about "hugging mother earth" or saving trees. I'm stretching the word ecology to mean how we are supposed to live in God's world for His glory. Some of these fourth-level questions are:

- What career should you have?
- Where should you live?
- What should you wear?

. . . and a host of other questions that surround living in God's world.

Sadly, this last question or problem typically gets the bulk of our attention. From the cradle to the grave, this is where most people spend the majority of their thinking time and physical energy. It is what Biff did until he came to that place, as a forty-one-year-old man, where he was totally disillusioned.

The Main Thing

My counsel to him was to forget about what he wanted to be when he grew up and begin unraveling the mysteries of God through a heartfelt pursuit of Him. The more he understands God and relates to Him correctly, the more he will understand himself.

The more he understands himself, the more he will be able to speak into his wife's life by serving her, maturing her, and being what God has called him to be for her (Ephesians 5:25–32). After his first three problems are moving in the right direction, his last problem will not be so daunting. It will be less of a burden to figure out what he should be doing with his life.

Call to Action

I do wonder how many people have spent most of their lives trying to resolve problem four—the cares of this life, only to be disillusioned because they negated the priorities of the first three problems. What about you? If you placed your problems in their order of importance to you, what would that tell you about yourself and your relationship with God?

1. How do you need to change?
2. What do you need to do first?

Chapter 6

Twelve Universal Assumptions

Traditional biblical counseling relies heavily on historical data as a way to find out about the person. The traditional biblical counselor uses assessments and other inventory style questions to gather information before meeting the counselee.

According to this conventional method of counseling, the counselor believes to have as much information before the person shows up for their counseling appointment is the best approach to care for them. The assumption is that understanding the person can be found in the history of the individual rather than the heart of the individual. That approach is different from the way Jesus practiced biblical counseling.

"But Jesus on his part did not entrust himself to them, because he knew all people and needed no one to bear witness about man, for he himself knew what was in man" (John 2:24–25).

Look Inside, Not Outside

Jesus already knew what the problems were before He met the person. The person's history, whatever that may be, did not alter what He already knew about him. If anything, it only affirmed what He already knew about the person because Jesus had inside information.

History and shaping influences were merely data points like a trail of breadcrumbs that allowed Jesus to show the person what He already knew. The difference between Jesus' model of soul care and the traditional biblical counselor is between being historically-centered or heart-centered.

Knowing the history of a person does play a role. I am not throwing the baby out with its history. Understanding a person's past provides the counselor the information needed to paint a clearer picture to help the counselee see how he thinks and makes decisions.

"The good person out of the good treasure of his heart produces good, and the evil person out of his evil treasure produces evil, for out of the abundance of the heart his mouth speaks" (Luke 6:45).

Jesus taught that there is no discontinuity between who a person is and what a person does. The heart causes the behavior, and the behavior reveals the heart. The primary key for any discipler is to have a thorough working knowledge of a person's heart. Christians do not need to be at a disadvantage in any counseling situation because, like Jesus, we know what is in man.

My History   My Narrative

My Life

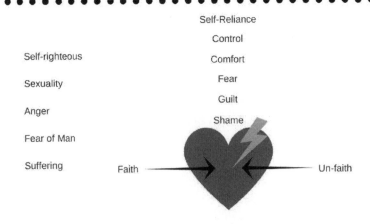

Self-Reliance

Control

Self-righteous   Comfort

Sexuality   Fear

                                        Guilt

Anger   Shame

Fear of Man

Suffering   Faith ——————→ ←—————— Un-faith

We understand the hearts of people—how they think, process, struggle, and respond to life's issues. Why? All individuals are the same where it matters. What the Christian needs more than historical data is a sound biblical heart hermeneutic.

Think of the infographic like the letter "V." At the top of the "V" are all people. Each one of them is a unique person with a unique story. They come from different places and are shaped by various things. Some of their main shaping influences are their DNA, parents, siblings, family dynamics, culture, education, religion, and friends. All of these things give them a one-of-a-kind story. It makes them who they are.

You'll notice how their stories echo the condition of their hearts, which is a commonality we all share. We're all cut from the same cloth. That cloth may have a unique behavioral history, but it still came from the same point of origin: Adam. We're all in and from one man. In that way none of us are unique. While we can be radically different on the outside, we cannot be entirely different on the inside. That would be an impossible counseling conundrum: seven billion people who function seven billion different ways with seven billion different control centers (hearts).

The Bible does not talk that way about humanity. When the Bible talks about how people function in their hearts, it uses a universal language. (cf. Romans 3:10–12, 23). If you begin to gather our everyday struggles together, you'll eventually have a list of themes that make up every person in the world.

As you move from our unique history to our shared problems, you will eventually cross a line (the dotted line in the infographic), which reveals a similar theme: your current disciple is like your last disciple. Our commonality is one of the many beautiful things about discipleship that gives any Christian a head start with the person he is discipling.

1. You don't need to be omniscient to help someone.

2. You don't need to have lived their lives to help them.

3. You are more common than uncommon where it matters.

4. You can relate to anyone, regardless of gender, age, or origin.

Our shared experiences are part of the explanation about Jesus' temptations being like our temptations (Hebrews 4:14–15). His temptations were not necessarily behavioral temptations like ours, but He was tempted in His heart like us, e.g., fear, anxiety, anger, self-reliance, craving for comfort, and ambition.

Counseling Adam

Let's pretend you are counseling Adam. Let's put him on the couch and diagnose his real problems, the ones in his heart. In the infographic, you'll notice there are two groups of heart problems. The first group begins with unbelief and moves vertically through self-reliance. The second group is on the left-hand side of the graphic and is more eclectic than sequential. Let's take the first group.

Unbelief – If you work a person down to their most fundamental and foundational problem, it will be unbelief. Not trusting God was the first sin of Adam, and all of the other sins flow out of this common heart commitment.

If we believed God the way we should, we would not sin the way we do. Adam trusted God in Genesis 1 and 2, and everything was copacetic. In Genesis 3 he decided not to trust God, and the drift from God began.

An example of basic unbelief is when I choose to get angry at my wife. In such a situation I'm no longer trusting the Lord, choosing rather to rely on myself. Another example is when I become impatient at the traffic patterns in my city. I'm no longer resting (trusting) in God's sovereign care for my life but demanding things go according to my plans. All sin, big or small, flows out of a heart of unbelief.

Shame – After Adam had chosen not to place his confidence (trust) in the Lord, he felt weird inside. His new condition is what we call biblical shame. It's an internal awkwardness where we're not entirely comfortable in our skins.

This uncomfortableness, if not satisfied by a redemptive relationship with the Lord, will motivate a person to find solace in other ways, through other means. Alternate approaches to feel good explain why so much unrest and discontentedness is in our lives.

Guilt – Born out of this shame comes the experience of guilt, which can be true or false guilt. Even unbelievers feel the guilt of their wrong actions (Romans 2:14–15). We're set up to feel guilty because we know there is something fundamentally broken inside of us (Romans 1:20). We're born in Adam. We have a sense of spiritual death (Romans 5:12).

Fear – The accumulative effect of the shame and guilt that stacks on top of our unbelief is fear. That is what Adam felt at the beginning of the fall. He said as much after the Lord questioned him about his unbelieving actions (Genesis 3:10). He intuitively knew he had done wrong. He felt the brokenness inside of him. Thus, he went for the leaf grab. Not being satisfied with just covering his shame, he bolted. He was running scared.

Comfort – Because his underlying sinful patterns were not rectified by the redemptive work of the cross through salvation and ongoing sanctification, he instinctively desired to find happiness through more man-centered means.

Rather than running back to God—the only solution for his problems—he continued to take matters into his hands (Ephesians 2:8–9). He became a comfort hoarder. Looking in the wrong places for what we want is our Adamic pattern, too. When things are going wonky, we find comfort outside of the Lord's means.

Control – Adam was now in control of his life. In most cases, we do not realize how often we succumb to control as a tool to solve our problems. It is so habitual and subtle. To trust ourselves rather than the Lord seems to make sense (Proverbs 14:12).

Even when the Lord writes personal suffering into our story (2 Corinthians 1:8–9 and 12:7–10), we resist by redoubling our efforts to seize control. At the core of our being, we don't want to rely on (trust) God. Unbelief is a problem that permeates all our relationships and contexts.

Self-Reliance – We can even feel justified in being self-reliant. The underlying fear is that we are not sure if the Lord has our backs. Or, maybe we know the Lord has our backs, but our intuition says that what He plans for us might not be what we want.

We know that if God was willing to put His Son to death (Isaiah 53:10), it is possible He could allow disappointing things in our lives too (Genesis 50:20). Our God is a radical God, who is not squeamish about giving us hard things for our good, His glory, and the benefit of others.

The Same Cloth

The most common themes you will find in people's lives are what I've outlined from the unbelief to self-reliance list in the infographic. As you listen to people's stories, you'll pick up on those themes. Some of the indicators will be more accentuated than others. It depends on the person.

What you'll see first is a self-reliant person who is having a hard time fully trusting the Lord in their unique situation. The process of self-reliance to unbelief is what their story will immediately tell you. And as you listen to them, you'll pick up on other underlying and hidden themes—more assumptions, if you will.

The second constellation of sin patterns in the infographic is not necessarily related to the first group. These things are eclectic. It's important to know these common patterns because you will interact with some or all of them every time you engage a person. Here's a quick glance at them in no particular order.

Dislike Suffering – We have a weak theology of suffering because we have an aversion to suffering. If we can get out of pain, we will take the quickest exit. An exit strategy may not be God's plan for our lives.

Self-Righteous – We all have a high view of ourselves. We are easily tempted to esteem ourselves more than others (Philippians 2:3–4).

Sinful Anger – The most common expression of self-righteousness is anger —a greater than/better than attitude that puts other people down. We live in a hostile world, and we're easily tempted to be angry.

Fear of Man – We're also insecure or have what the Bible calls fear of man (Proverbs 29:25). We are afraid of being hurt and rejected by others. The greater this fear is, the more other people will have control over our lives.

Sexuality Issues – We are a sexually messed up lot. I'll not make a case for this since it's understood, and there is much information in cyberspace about this common universal problem.

Call to Action

These twelve universal assumptions are part of every person's life. Depending on your story, you will find them peeking out of your heart, too. These are some of the common themes in man (John 2:24–25). It is what was in Adam, and God cut you from the same cloth. The real question is whether you can see these things in your life. The more effectively you can counsel yourself, the more effectively you'll be able to care for others.

1. In what ways are you self-reliant?
2. In what ways do you seek to control your life?
3. In what ways are you a comfort seeker?
4. In what ways do you fear?

5. In what ways do you struggle with internal shame and guilt?

6. In what ways is unbelief active in your life?

Chapter 7

Why Do I Do That?

None of us are perfect, and most of us have a better version of ourselves that we would like to become. Dissatisfaction with self is why one of the most common discipleship questions is, "How can I change?"

Sometimes the discipler will provide simple answers, such as trust God, let go and let God, or you need to repent. In most cases, these cliché-type answers are not helpful. In some situations, they do more harm than good. No Christian should make change the only possibility for a person who desires a more preferred iteration of themselves. That kind of hope is not in the Christian's toolbox or within the Christian's ability to accomplish.

"But he said to me, 'My grace is sufficient for you, for my power is made perfect in weakness.' Therefore I will boast all the more gladly of my weaknesses, so that the power of Christ may rest upon me" (2 Corinthians 12:9).

What the Christian should suggest is that regardless of what you may be going through, there is grace for your situation. This kind of advice fits well within the Christian's offerings for the sad soul.

I am curious.

1. Do you have a personal problem you would like to see changed?
2. If you chose counseling as an option, would a change be the only acceptable solution?
3. How loosely do you hold the possibility of never changing?

Let's take a look at a typical situation and work through the possible complexities of why people are the way they are. I am going to use depression for this case study. You can insert any problem into this analysis and filter it through the process that I am going to provide for you.

I will assume you have read the previous chapters in this book. If so, you are in the best possible place to figure out why you are the way you are or why you do what you do. With those chapters as the context for change, let's proceed.

I Am Depressed

Sam struggles with depression. He has been this way for as long as he can remember. He comes to me for help because he wants to change. Transformation is a good desire, and I want to help him change, assuming that is God's pleasure for him.

Though I know I cannot offer Sam the hope of changing in the way he may want it, I can give him some helpful ways to think about and respond to his depression. I can also let him know how God's grace is sufficient for him, regardless of the outcome of our time together (2 Corinthians 12:9).

My goal is not to give Sam false hope. I want to offer biblical hope. I want to encourage him but not set him up for future disappointment. Christians must be careful from falsely presenting the Lord or falsely presenting the sufficiency of God's Word. Christians must be honest with those within their care, which means walking through all possible outcomes for the script the Lord is writing.

After Sam rightly establishes his thoughts in the Lord as the only answer and the Bible as the most effective system of thought for problem-solving, I want to lay down two other essential tenets for problem-solving. They are:

1. I do not know why he is depressed.
2. All of his problems relate to sin in some way.

This first tenet is my desire to be honest with him while resisting personal arrogance or false hope. It would be arrogant of me to tell him why he is depressed. Trying to explain his depression entirely could circumvent the complexity of his problem as well as the mysteries of the Lord.

"The secret things belong to the LORD our God, but the things that are revealed belong to us and to our children forever, that we may do all the words of this law" (Deuteronomy 29:29).

Think about this for a moment: There is an element of mystery to our problems. Can a grasshopper discern the ways of a man? Can a finite man understand the ways of infinite God?

"It is he who sits above the circle of the earth, and its inhabitants are like grasshoppers" (Isaiah 40:22).

If you are not comfortable with the elements of mystery when it comes to your problems, you will never be comfortable with your problems or your God. Where were you when God laid the foundations of the earth (Job 38:4)?

We must be careful that we do not boast in our arrogance, thinking we have a complete understanding of our problems. We do not (James 4:16). I want to inform Sam how the divine mysteries of His will are unsearchable and how the depths of His ways are not within our scope of discovery or comprehension (Isaiah 40:28).

I also want him to have a measure of comfortableness when it comes to problem-solving. Part of this comfortableness will come if he can rest in the mysteries of God's will. There is blessedness and hope in our ignorance if we can rest in the Lord to navigate our circumstances from His sovereign perspective.

Problems Are Related to Sin

My second statement can be frustrating to some people while too simplistic to others. I understand. There is a tendency with some, especially the science-centered or education-centered camps, to reject that which does not sound sophisticated.

Our culture's poorly positioned emphasis on science and education has partially shaped us to be ignorant of the truth of God's Word. In a way, it is humorous. In a way, it is sad. It is also ironic that our infatuation with education as the solution to our problems has made us more ignorant than we know.

"If anyone imagines that he knows something, he does not yet know as he ought to know" (1 Corinthians 8:2).

"For the foolishness of God is wiser than men, and the weakness of God is stronger than men" (1 Corinthians 1:25).

God is not embarrassed about offering simple answers, and neither am I.

"For it is written, 'I will destroy the wisdom of the wise, and the discernment of the discerning I will thwart.' Where is the one who is wise? Where is the scribe? Where is the debater of this age? Has not God made foolish the wisdom of the world?" (1 Corinthians 1:19–20).

It is good for the Lord to make things simple by placing them on a lower shelf. Though we might not like the idea of admitting our ignorance, there is freedom, strength, humility, and wisdom in embracing our weaknesses (2 Corinthians 4:7).

The Main Thing

The main culprit for why Sam is depressed is sin. When Adam and Eve disobeyed God in the garden of Eden, they were cursed by God (Genesis 2:16–17). Their disobedience meant they were totally cursed—organically and nonorganically.

It is called total depravity. There was no stone left unturned because of the curse God placed on humanity. Every part of our being was affected—spiritually and physically. Depravity makes sin the source of Sam's depression. It cannot be any other way. For Sam to grasp this simple idea, he must think comprehensively about the doctrine of sin. For example, I am not saying he has necessarily done anything wrong. The act of being born set him up for brokenness.

"Who can bring a clean thing out of an unclean? There is not one" (Job 14:4).

Think of sin like a drop of dye placed in a beaker of water. Once the drop hits the water, the entire beaker is contaminated. The chances of Sam being messed up at birth is 100 percent.

"Therefore, just as sin came into the world through one man, and death through sin, and so death spread to all men because all sinned" (Romans 5:12).

Every person comes into the world with unique and specific sinful tendencies. It is as random as there are people. Individual brokenness is why the gay guy can say, "I was born this way." Maybe he was born that way. I was born with my weaknesses, shortcomings, and sinful proclivities.

Everybody is born that way. To say, "I was born that way" is merely affirming the Bible's declaration that everyone has sinned and fallen short of

God's glory (Romans 3:23). I do not argue with the gay guy, who says he was born that way. I agree with him. The impasse comes when he uses his brokenness as an excuse to stay broken. He misses the point of the gospel, which is transformation.

Sam came into the world in a contaminated beaker. He received what we all received. There are many things wrong with him. You see this idea in 1 Thessalonians 5:14 where Paul exhorts us to encourage the fainthearted. The word fainthearted means small-soul. There are people with little souls. We all have different soul capacities. Could it be that God gave Sam a small soul, which makes him unable to live in a similar victory like a large soul individual? I honestly do not know.

Process of Elimination

What I want to do with a person like Sam is to begin working through all the possibilities regarding what can make a person depressed. Though he can alter some of these things, there will be other issues harder to transform. Sam may be like the gay guy—he was born that way. Sam will have to be taught the primary purpose of his unique brokenness—to glorify God in whatever condition he finds himself (Philippians 4:10–13).

The Lord's primary point for Sam's brokenness is to teach him to rely on God rather than himself (2 Corinthians 1:8–9, 4:7, and 12:7–10). The gay guy will use his brokenness as an excuse to live in sin. Perchance God gave Sam a proclivity to be depressed, he must see it as his opportunity to glorify God.

1. The Lord permitted Joni Eareckson Tada to be a quadriplegic.
2. The Lord permitted me to be divorced.
3. The Lord permitted William Cowper to struggle with depression.
4. The Lord permitted His Son to die on a cross (Isaiah 53:10).

Sometimes the Lord will give us unalterable problems. The four issues I listed above are physical, relational, spiritual, and sacrificial—in that order.

1. All of them were unalterable.
2. All of them were related to sin.
3. All of them were the will of God.
4. All of them were for God's glory.

We must factor in these possibilities. Typically, when we think about our problems, we do not consider the possibility of God's will being contrary to our preferences (Luke 22:42).

The way you discern if your situation is unchangeable is by eliminating all the other possibilities. I am going to list for you some of the things Sam needs to consider regarding his depression. The list is in a random, eclectic order. All of the items can cause some people to be depressed. Some of these things Sam can change, while others he will not be able to alter.

Organic or Physical Issues

1. Is he overweight?
2. Does he smoke?
3. Does he drink alcohol?
4. Is he on medication?
5. Does he exercise?
6. Is he disciplined? Does he go to bed on time and get up on time?
7. Does he eat healthily?
8. Does he drink healthily?
9. What is his IQ?
10. Does he have physical disabilities?

Nonorganic or Spiritual Issues

1. Is he a Christian?

2. Does he have a hidden sin?

3. Is his conscience hard, weak, confused, commingled?

4. Is he regularly encouraged by God's Word?

5. Is he regularly helped through prayer?

6. What does he think about himself?

7. Is he closing, maintaining, or widening the gap between himself and Jesus?

8. How does he respond to pressures and challenges?

9. What would make him happy?

10. How mature is he in his faith?

11. How does he think about God?

Relational Issues

1. Does he live in a supportive community?

2. Is he free to be himself?

3. Is he regularly encouraged by others?

4. Does he attend a biblical church?

5. Is he a servant?

6. Is he an encourager?

7. How do his primary relationships treat him?

8. Is he teachable?

9. Is he humble?

10. Is he correctable?

11. Is he easy to befriend?

Everything in these lists contributes to depression, as well as exacerbate depression if they go unchanged. How they interrelate to Sam will give clues to his depression. It's essential to work with Sam in thinking through how these things may tempt him toward depression or cause him to be depressed. Then you want to begin eliminating the ones that tempt him.

Sam will be able to change many of the things in these lists, assuming they need changing. Before you conclude his depression is unalterable, you want to make sure he is doing all he can do to change. Often a person will plead ignorance as to why he is depressed and then as you unpack his life, according to some of the questions in my list, you realize he is more culpable than he is admitting to or is aware.

If he is serious about changing, he needs to address each item, while adding to the lists. If he has done this and is living honestly before God and others, it could be there will always be a temptation toward depression. At this point, you would want to begin discipling him regarding God's all-sufficient grace for an unchangeable situation. It could be the Lord seeks to magnify Himself through Sam's weakness. Carefully read 2 Corinthians 1:8–9, 4:7, and 12:7–10.

Call to Action

1. Will you work through the lists in this chapter, answering all the questions that apply to your struggle? How did you do?
2. What is one thing or one area in your life that you would like to change?
3. Do you believe it can change? Why did you answer that way?
4. What needs to happen to glorify the Lord through your weaknesses?

Chapter 8

When I Kept Silent

Are you more concerned about what God thinks about your sin or what others may think about your sin? Your thoughts about this crucial question will determine the quality of your life. The way you can know the answer to what controls your heart is by measuring your willingness (or unwillingness) to share your faults, failures, and sins with other "appropriate" people.

I did not say you should share your sin broadly; I said your willingness (or unwillingness) to share the condition of your life and relationships with other people would determine who or what has the most control over you.

If God's opinion of you has the most control over your life, you have your answer: you are a humble, God-centered, God-glorifying, sin-mortifying, Christlike example, who is more concerned with Christ's reputation than your own. But if you are more concerned with what others think about you, to the point that you are motivated to hide sin, you are in more trouble than you could ever imagine.

When I Kept Silent

King David lived both ways. After he had committed adultery, he began to cover his tracks. David did this for about a year. Because he was not willing to come clean regarding his sin, the Lord did for him what he was not going to do for himself. He sent Nathan to break his heart and expose his deception.

Before Nathan's visit, David commented on what his life was like when he tried to bury the sin he had committed. If this is you, read carefully. Listen to King David.

"For when I kept silent, my bones wasted away through my groaning all day long. For day and night your hand was heavy upon me; my strength was dried up as by the heat of summer" (Psalm 32:3–4).

If this passage does not put the fear of God in you, perhaps you are in a near helpless condition. For nearly twelve months David lied and connived, pretending all was well when it was not. He was trying to ignore what he did, as well as the One who could see into the darkness of his heart.

"And no creature is hidden from his sight, but all are naked and exposed to the eyes of him to whom we must give account" (Hebrews 4:13).

There is only one way for you to escape from what has captured your heart; it is through the door of humility, confession, honesty, and transparency. You and I can fake out each other, but you cannot deceive the Lord. And even if you could keep the illusion going for a season, there would eventually be a payday someday. The longer you resist the truth, by holding on to lies, the more complicated your life and relationships will become.

Pushing Truth Aside

"For the wrath of God is revealed from heaven against all ungodliness and unrighteousness of men, who by their unrighteousness suppress the truth" (Romans 1:18).

Paul gives more insight into what David was experiencing when he laid out the degenerating process to the Romans of what happens when a person attempts to press the truth of God out of their lives. He talked about how God's wrath—His angry displeasure—would rain down from heaven on anyone who lived in ungodly and unrighteous ways. He said this happened when people volitionally chose to press the truth of God from their lives.

68

To suppress the truth is to press it out of your life. It is like pushing down on a balloon filled with water. The water shifts to the right and the left. It distorts what was once normal. When you press the truth of God from your life, by holding on to or propagating deception, you will have a distorted soul. You cannot exchange the truth of God for a lie while worshipping the creature more than the Creator, and expect distortion not to happen (Romans 1:25).

David did this though he knew the truth about God. He was a man after the Lord's heart (1 Samuel 13:14), but he chose a path of sin. The sadness is not so much about the way of sin (adultery) he chose, which is bad enough, but the deception he propagated after he sinned—a process that began to break down his body and soul. How could it be any other way?

Dulling the Inner Voice

"Today, if you hear his voice, do not harden your hearts" (Hebrews 4:7).

In Hebrews, you learn even more about how ongoing and unrepented sin has a dulling effect on your inner being. Do you see the downward progression of the person who refuses to deal rightly with sin? While the physical debilitation that David went through was horrible enough, it was the dulling of his conscience that may have been the worst of all.

The conscience (Latin: co-knowledge) is your inner voice. Your conscience is your moral thermostat that tells you when you are doing what is right or wrong. If your inner voice becomes dull of hearing (Hebrews 5:11), you are unhooking yourself from the morality of God, while choosing a path that is wise in your own eyes (Isaiah 5:21). Paul said people like this were not wise, but fools (Romans 1:22).

To be disconnected from God's morality with no moral compass releases you to be a god of your life (Proverbs 14:12). The worst case of this in the Bible is Lucifer. Though no one will do what he did, there are no known limits

69

as to what a depraved soul can do without God's restrictions. Sometimes people ask,

"Can you believe what [so and so] did?" Almost without exception, I say, "I can believe it. If [so and so] has been living apart from God in a self-absorbed way, I am surprised you are surprised by their actions."

Paul talked about this to his young protegé, Timothy, as he was teaching him about what could happen when deceitfulness and insincerity were in play. He said people who participated in such things would sear their consciences (1 Timothy 4:2). The seared conscience is equivalent to the cattleman placing an orange-hot iron brand on the cow's rump to the point of searing its hide. The seared spot does not have feeling. Callousness is a dangerous thing when it happens to a person's conscience.

David was heading that way. He was willfully exchanging the truth of God for a lie, and he was not about to alter his course. Fortunately, there was someone who loved him enough to do for him what he was not going to do for himself.

Enter Nathan.

Turn On the Light

The Lord nudged Nathan to go to his friend. You know the story. One of the things so amazing about this story is that David did not get the point of Nathan's fictitious monologue (2 Samuel 12:1–6). Nathan was talking, and David was not hearing (Matthew 11:15). He was so blind, so detached, so dull, and so determined to hide his sin that he did not have ears to hear or eyes to see.

"Nathan said to David, 'You are the man!'" (2 Samuel 12:7a).

Nathan stopped beating around the bush with his sheep story and spoke plainly to David. Never underestimate the hardening process of the conscience when a person refuses to own their sin. Do not expect them to see what is right in front of them.

The reason it is as plain as the nose on your face is because you are walking in the light. Light does that to a person. Any person, including Christians, can walk in darkness. John reminded Christians of this truth when he talked about how sin can complicate the Christian's life.

"But if we walk in the light, as he is in the light, we have fellowship with one another, and the blood of Jesus his Son cleanses us from all sin. If we say we have no sin, we deceive ourselves, and the truth is not in us" (1 John 1:7–8).

David was essentially saying, "I have no sin," and John would say back to him, "You have deceived yourself, and the truth is not in you." That is why David could not understand what Nathan was trying to accomplish.

If you are sitting around waiting for a person—who is willfully pressing the truth of God out of their lives—to come clean, you may not only be sitting around for a long time, but you may be culpable. You could be enabling them in their sin because you did not speak the truth to them—the truth they could not see because they turned off the light in their souls.

- Do not underestimate the power of sin.
- Do not underestimate what it can do to a person's conscience.
- Do not think you have no moral responsibility to bring the light to them so they can see.

71

Hurt Your Friend

"Faithful are the wounds of a friend; profuse are the kisses of an enemy" (Proverbs 27:6).

Wounding David was the kindest thing Nathan could do for his friend. Saying hard things reminds me of my favorite quote from my former professor, Wayne Mack. He said, when thinking about doing hard things to someone,

"You can hate me now and love me later, or you can love me now and hate me later."

I doubt David ever hated Nathan for what he did, but there is no question that Nathan brought pain into David's life. Nathan loved him so much that he had no choice but to hurt his friend. If you logically follow the downward progression David presented in Psalm 32:3–4, there seems to be little question that David was deteriorating physically and spiritually by the day.

David's confession in that Psalm reads like he would not have lived much longer. Things went wrong quickly for David. It was God's mercy imposing itself in David's life by sending someone to wound him. He was impulsive to react to Nathan's sheep story, but when he found out he was the main character of the story, he shut his mouth (Job 40:4–5). Without interruption, he let his friend speak.

The fantastic news is once his eyes were open, the spirit quickened, and he knew immediately what he had done and how he needed to respond. When Nathan finished, David said the only thing that needed to be said.

"I have sinned against the LORD" (2 Samuel 12:13a).

Will You Choose Life?

Six words summed it up. There was nothing else to say because nothing else mattered at that moment. It is true that David sinned against more people than the Lord, but at that moment, there was only one thing that mattered. This brings us around to my opening statement:

Are you more concerned about what God thinks about your sin or what others may think about your sin? Your thoughts about this crucial question will determine the quality of your life. The way you can know the answer to what controls your heart is by measuring your willingness (or unwillingness) to share your faults, failures, and sins with other "appropriate" people.

After David had sinned, he plotted a deceptive plan to cover up his actions. He hurt many people in the process. The only thing that mattered was for others to not know what he did. It was a bold move for someone who was after the Lord's heart. How could someone be so connected to God and be so self-deceived?

David's life is a call for you to do reflective self-examination. If someone who loved God so much could fall so far, how much more possible is it for you or me to detach our hearts from the truth we know?

While his adultery was horrendous and his deception was causing physical and spiritual suicide, the amazing thing about this story is his restoration. Like the prodigal son, the only thing that mattered to him was restoration (Luke 15:17–22). You will be able to discern a person's sincerity by the radicalness of their repentance. The prodigal son clearly threw in the white towel and gave up all control of his life to his father. David did similarly.

I am not suggesting that you broadcast your sin to the world, but I am suggesting that you be willing to do anything it takes to restore what sin destroyed. In David's case, you see how he walked out his repentance: he broadcasted it to the world. (Read Psalm 32:1–11 and Psalm 51:1–19.)

Call to Action

The most effective way for you to test the genuineness of your repentance is by giving up control of the situation to those whom you trust and who have proven themselves faithful to the practical applications of God's Word in your life.

If your so-called repentance is more about controlling the outcomes, you are not in a "repenting frame of mind." But if you are willing to give up control of your life and your situation by humbly submitting to those who can help you, then expect God's amazing favor in your life (James 4:6).

1. How silent are you about your sin?
2. Why are you afraid to share your struggles?
3. What are you trying to protect?
4. What are you trying to control?
5. Are you willing to bury your actions and reap the consequences, regardless of what they may be?
6. Or, will you listen to Nathan and respond like David?

"Blessed is the one whose transgression is forgiven, whose sin is covered. Blessed is the man against whom the LORD counts no iniquity, and in whose spirit there is no deceit" (Psalm 32:1–2).

Chapter 9

Two Essentials to Change

Transformation does not happen automatically or miraculously. If you want to change, you will have to challenge yourself at the deepest and most difficult level of your soul, and the two most fearsome hurdles you'll have to cross are honesty and transparency.

1. Are you willing to be honest about yourself with others?
2. Are you willing to be transparent about yourself with others?

A counseling office is a place where people are tempted to tell lies. I have said that counseling is a lying profession. If you don't struggle with folks lying to you, become a counselor. I am telling you the truth. Let me illustrate with two fictional but common stories I have heard from counselees.

Biff and Mable were driving to their counseling session strategizing on what they were going to say to me. The drive was more like a bartering session. Biff was appealing to Mable to not tell about the night of December 14. Mable was threatening to tell me if he did not commit to at least five counseling sessions. Biff committed to five meetings.

Bud and Marge were barterers, too. This time it was Marge who was doing the bartering. She is hyper-insecure and did not want me to know that they had sex before marriage. Bud did not want me to know either, so he promised not to tell.

Biff, Mable, Bud, and Marge predetermined what they would and would not say before they came to my office to ask me if I would help them through their marriage problems. Read that last sentence again. Do you see anything wrong with it? They wanted my help, but they predetermined to hide some of the facts.

Let's suppose you went to an emergency room, but you decided before entering the hospital to withhold certain pieces of information about what was wrong with you. Do you see a problem with that strategy?

The two fictional scenarios regularly happen in my office. I have to dig, pull, plead, and appeal for people to tell the truth. It should not be this way. Too often people come to counseling afraid to tell the truth. It's a self-defeating approach that hinders the opportunity for change to happen.

Honesty Requires Transparency

Will you be honest with me? I mean, will you be really, really honest with me? I am not talking about telling the truth as much as I am talking about being transparent? Will you be transparent with me? Honesty is about telling the truth and telling truthful facts. Transparency is about being open and honest with all the facts, especially the facts that relate to why the person is not changing.

1. The honest person with marriage problems will say he has marriage problems.

2. The transparent person will say he has marriage problems, and he will tell you how he is specifically contributing to the marriage problems.

Have you ever had a person tell you about the problems they were going through, but as you were listening to them, you were thinking they were not telling the whole truth? They were not transparent about themselves. In most cases, they were telling the truth about the other person while not being transparent about themselves.

Biff is great about telling the truth regarding his marriage problems, but he is horrible about opening up and being transparent about how he is repeatedly sabotaging his marriage. He says, "I'm telling the truth" as though he is pleading a case. The truth is that he is telling the truth. The truth is also that he is not honest with all of the facts because he is not transparent about himself.

If he were transparent about himself, he would be self-disclosing, a truth that could potentially reconcile his marriage. Biff is not as much interested in reconciling his marriage as he is in winning an argument, protecting his reputation, and satisfying his long overdue desire to punish his wife by highlighting her sins to me.

Mable, his wife, is guilty of what she did, but Biff is guilty, too. His unwillingness to tip the scales toward his culpability while focusing mostly on her sins does not help the reconciliation process. He is harboring bitterness in his heart because he is hurt. He is also angry and unforgiving, which is the transparent truth that he hides behind all his truth-telling. If he decides to repent of his lack of transparency rather than punishing his wife for her sins, the whole truth will be out, and they may be able to reconcile.

Diversionary Tactics

It is easy to get caught up in the drama of life, which sometimes mutes the real issues that are happening. Sometimes getting caught up in the drama of life is intentional so that some of the facts stay hidden. Keeping the drama stirred up and putting the weight of the problems on the other person, like what Biff was doing, becomes a distraction that keeps him from being confronted by the things he needs to change.

Secret keeping has a deteriorating effect on the guilty conscience because the hidden truth gnaws at the soul. It is like pretending the cancer that is eating away your body does not exist. Unwillingness to acknowledge sinfulness does not stop it from damaging you or your relationships. It is tempting to divert the conversation to side-track redemptive efforts.

Marge was like this. She was frustrated with Bud because he was annoying and a general pain to be around. The whole truth is that Marge was a pain, too. In the depths of her soul, she knew something inside of her was wrong, but she did not want to own it. She muted the inward gnawing by keeping the blame on

Bud. Like Biff, she was not an honest person because of her lack of transparency.

At other times, she would fill her days with enough activities to ignore the unresolved guilt and shame she felt. The real truth about her marriage was not so much about what Bud was doing. The issue she needed to deal with first was in her heart. I pleaded with her, "Will you confront yourself and, maybe for the first time in a long time, be honest with yourself?"

I gave her a list of things she could do to practice truth-telling, which meant being honest and transparent. This practice would be good for anyone who struggles with being transparent.

1. Talk to God.
2. Tell Him that you are struggling.
3. Let Him know that you are afraid to be transparent.
4. Ask Him to help you (James 4:6).
5. Practice discerning when the Spirit is appealing to you to be truthful.
6. Respond in those Spirit-illuminated moments by being honest and transparent (James 4:17).

Another Angle to Transparency

1. Wouldn't it be nice if some of your relationships were more open?
2. Wouldn't it be nice to have at least one person that you could communicate with transparently?
3. How do the consequences of Adam's sin—hiding behind fig leaves—affect you?

Recently, someone asked me if it was wise for a person to tell his spouse everything he was thinking. My answer to the question was "no" and "yes." I could not answer the question in the black-and-white way in which it was asked. For example, at the beginning of my relationship with my wife, there were many things I did not tell her. I did not tell her that I thought she was hot. I do tell her now.

Relationships begin with discretion and ignorance. You do not say everything you're thinking about another person. That's discretion. You do not know all that can be known about the other person. That's ignorance. Strong relationships cross both of those barriers. As you move closer to each other, you learn more about each other. You're also less discreet. A good marriage should always be moving toward oneness, which cannot happen without honesty and transparency.

No relationship is static. We are either moving toward unity or away from it. Either we are moving toward more in-depth community (koinonia), or we are not. The implication of the word community expects communication that is growing progressively deeper and more transparent.

Transparency Illustrated

My wife knows I can be tempted to lust after other women, which is why she becomes an additional set of eyes for me. For example, when we are at the beach, she is kind and humble enough to serve me by thinking through where we put our blankets and other paraphernalia.

This is a kindness from the Lord to have such a humble complementer (Genesis 2:18). It would be sad and lonely to have a helper that I could not talk to about the sinful inner workings of my soul. Being open and honest with each other are core components to strong relationships. These relationships do not just happen. It takes work that is always founded on the gospel.

The closer you draw to the Lord, the greater the desire will be to become closer to others. If you choose to drift from the Lord like what Adam did, it will create a proportional distance in your other relationships. Sin divides, causes disunity, and keeps you hiding in the bushes, wrapped in fig leaves (Genesis 3:7–8).

To pursue sanctification is to seek God in the context of community. The more you walk in His light, the more open and honest you will be with others (1 John 1:7–10). You can discern a person's relationship with God by how they are sharing Him in a community.

Build a Bridge

Perhaps you're helping someone who is not responding to your care. Sometimes the relationship is not secure enough to where you can dig a little deeper with the individual. Here is a truth that has served me over the years when I am in similar situations: You build relational bridges to carry truth over to people.

If there is no relational bridge, it will be hard to be honest with someone because of the imminent danger of offending them, pressing them too soon, or scaring them away. But if you have favor with them and there is a carefully constructed relational bridge, you may be able to carry even difficult truth to them. It will require you to weigh and measure the truth you want to communicate. As you know, it takes time to build a sufficient bridge that will allow you to speak the whole truth to a person.

We typically know more than we say because there is not a complete bridge to communicate everything you're thinking about a person. What you do not want to do is communicate truth prematurely. Jesus even withheld the whole truth because His disciples were not able to receive all that He knew about His mission.

Slow down, be patient, and build trust in the relationship. If you do have favor with a friend, be honest with them while continuing to seek to be more frank with them. Tell them the truth, as much as you can and when you can. You will have to be the judge of how much truth you share and when you share it.

Here are two things to consider when speaking the truth in love to another person, especially when the communication bridge is not fortified (Ephesians 4:15).

First – If someone is wrong, they need to know what they are doing wrong, as well as the repercussions of their actions. The first repercussion is that they are defaming God's name because it's His name on the line, not ours (Psalm 23:3). If our actions are not making God's name great, we need friends who love us enough to let us know (Galatians 6:1–2).

Second – There will be times a person is unwilling to change because the Lord has not granted repentance to them (2 Timothy 2:24–25). Even so, this should not deter you from speaking the truth in love. Perhaps they will change in the future. You may want to give them the truth before they are ready to receive it, and when the time comes to apply it, they will appreciate your previous kindness to them.

Call to Action

1. Are you an honest person with those who are closest to you?
2. Are you a transparent person with those who are closest to you?
3. Do you know the difference between being honest and transparent and how the differences manifest in your life?
4. Are you willing to share these things with a close friend and appeal to them to speak into your life?

Chapter 10

The Control of Others

Being controlled by the opinion of other people is a problem every person struggles with to varying degrees. Biblically it is called fear of man. This term is typically more recognizable by such labels as the following:

Shyness	Insecurity	Peer Pressure	Codependency
Confrontational	Avoidance	Fear of Failure	Controller
Can't Lose	Gossip	Self-conscious	Embarrasses
Reactionary	Hates Rejection	Sensitive	Worrier

"The fear of man lays a snare, but whoever trusts in the LORD is safe" (Proverbs 29:25).

Like many of the verses in Proverbs, there is a parallel format: two lines, one stacked on top of the other. The first one is usually negative and the second one is positive. If you were to diagram the two lines, it could look something like the infographic on the next page. Notice the parallel in the infographic.

Snare or Safe?

In the diagram, you see the starting point as a heart of fear. When this happens, there is only one result—a snare (Galatians 6:1). Though your goal may be to be safe, you cannot get there from a heart of fear. Fear always leads to enslavement, not safety in Christ. To be safe and secure you have to deal with the heart of the problem first, which is your fear. Within the human heart, there is always a tension between fear and faith. When fear wins out, the person will struggle with various forms of insecurity. The insecure person wants to be safe but is held back by a fear of other people.

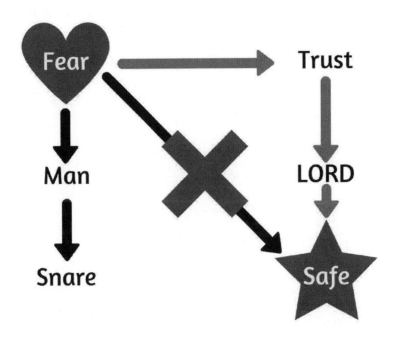

- Will they hurt me?
- Will they reject me?
- Will they like me?

As the person becomes more securely established in the Lord or at least when they become characterized and controlled by faith, the Lord will be large and safety will be assured.

I say "characterized by faith" because none of us live perfectly in faith. We regularly oscillate from fear to faith and back to fear again. No one has perfect, uninterrupted faith, though our general disposition should be faith in God. The two "people" in the preceding infographic are other people (man) and the Lord. When sinful fear is operative in the heart, the person will be influenced and controlled by others.

When faith is operative in the heart, the person will be primarily influenced and controlled by the Lord. It is our choice as to who or what will influence and control our thoughts. We are not victims, though we can feel more victimized than empowered when around certain people. If that is the case with you, please find help. Being manipulated by others is not what the Lord wants for you.

Matters of the Heart

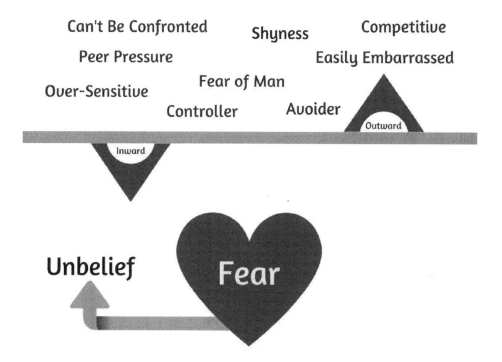

When you are addressing a fear of man issue, it is important to address it at its root. Though you will perceive the manifestations of fear in the outward behaviors, its roots will not be as evident because they are in the heart. If you do not take the fear out of its root, it will continue to resurface throughout a person's life. Heart theology is a basic understanding of how sanctification works.

Do not be fooled when you see the manifestations of fear in a person's behavior. Outward behaviors mean the motivations of the heart are entangled (James 1:14–15). Though I am talking about fear in the heart, you want to address the real culprit, which is unbelief.

Whenever fear rears its sinister head, it means the person is not trusting God. Fear thrives in the soil of unbelief. This kind of disbelief does not mean the person is an unbeliever. It could mean the person is an unbelieving believer (Mark 9:24) or practical atheist. Believe it or not, believing Christians struggle with unbelief, and when they do, fear will be entangling the heart.

Will You Like Me?

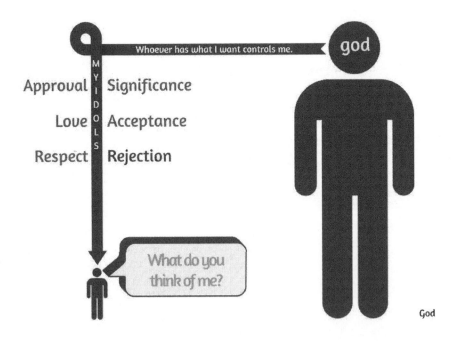

In real life what you will see is something like what the preceding infographic represents. The fear-motivated person will be looking for approval from someone. It does not mean they will be looking for approval from everyone. Fear of man is not an across-the-board, I-am-afraid-of-everyone kind of sin. You can be free from some relationships, but if in others you find yourself craving approval, acceptance, and respect. Or the other side of the craving coin, which is a fear of being rejected.

Perhaps you have friends with whom you are entirely comfortable, but then there are others who tempt you to crave their approval (or you fear their rejection). In such cases, they control you. The graphic is analogous to a marionette who is controlled by the strings of those we want to accept us. The real idolatry in the infographic is not the big person. The big person is merely the idol carrier—the one who can give you what you want. I listed some of those idols for you.

These are synonyms: approval, significance, love, acceptance, respect, and rejection are six ways of saying the same thing. You can pick the one that speaks most closely to your heart. As you glance to the bottom right of the infographic, you will notice the biggest problem of all. Can you see the word God? The smallness of the word contradicts the bigness of the problem. A small God leaves room for a heart to fear.

There is something broken in the heart of the person with a little God. There is a distortion as they experience, understand, discern, think about, and know God. This condition is a theological breakdown or what I call a small God disorder. What began as shyness, introversion, or peer pressure has now been diagnosed as a weak to a nonexistent relationship with the Lord. It is important to see this major problem with God.

The issue is not primarily about other people; it is about God. If this issue cannot be discerned and diagnosed, it will be impossible to change. Let me say it this way: if you do not know what to put off, this essential first step to the change process will keep you from ever being free (Ephesians 4:22).

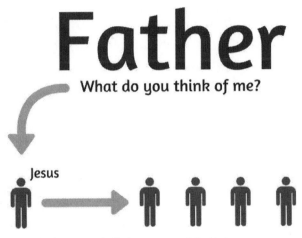

Father
What do you think of me?

Jesus

Now that I am not afraid of you, I can biblically love you.

The solution is not for the person to become bigger through an elevated self-esteem. The people who are wrapped up in fear of man spend too much time thinking about themselves. Thinking about themselves is their preoccupation, so to think more about themselves will only further their enslavement.

- How do I look?
- Will he like me?
- What are they thinking?
- Did I say it right?
- How did I come across?

Fear always leads to morbid self-evaluation and introspection. Rather than being preoccupied with self-estimation, it would better to esteem God and others more (Philippians 2:3–4).

The goal is to have a bigger God, which means bringing people down to size. No person should have manipulative power over someone else, even though we too often give that power to others. When we crave things like approval, acceptance, love, or respect from people, we will allow them to have the ability to control us. To change requires a reorientation of the mind: the only opinion in the world that should control us is God's opinion.

What do you need? What drives your cravings? What makes you tick? Do you need people's approval? The way you answer these questions will determine how you will relate to others and how you will live your life within those relationships. Either you will live to please people, or you will live in the freedom that God provides through His gospel.

- If you need people, you will suck them dry, and your relationships will always be strained or fractured.

- If you do not need people, you will be released to love and serve them the way Jesus did.

You will notice I inserted the name Jesus in the infographic because He is a perfect representation of what life looks like when the Lord controls you rather than others. Though He was despised and rejected by men, other people did not control Him with their disapproval (Isaiah 53:2–3). The opinion of His Father controlled Him, and we know how the Lord thought about Him. The Father's love for Jesus was off the charts. Mark described the dynamic relationship between the Father and the Son this way,

"And a voice came from heaven, 'You are my beloved Son; with you I am well pleased'" (Mark 1:11).

The Father was perfectly pleased with Jesus. He could do no wrong. The Pharisees and other knuckle-headed people could say and do all kinds of things to Jesus, but He would not allow them to control Him. He moved through our world unbothered and untethered by what man could do to Him. He was a man under the authority of Almighty God. That is your goal. If you place your faith appropriately in the Lord, you will not be controlled or manipulated by what others may try to do to you.

Free from the power of other people is the only way to live. Imagine being completely untethered from the opinion of others. This kind of experience with God is one of my lifelong goals regarding my sanctification. I long to be truly free in Christ. Jesus was 100 percent untethered from others, but He was not distant from or rude to others. He was free from others, but He was not apathetic about the depraved condition of others.

Being free from the opinion of people and caring deeply about people is perfect relational symmetry. There is no contradiction here. Not controlled but always loving is the only way you can fully, faithfully, and successfully pull off the two greatest commandments (Matthew 22:36–40).

Free Indeed

Submitting yourself to God is the only option you have if you want to be mature. Either other people will capture your heart because of your desire to be accepted, or you will be resting in the truth that God's opinion of you is positive, unchanging, and satisfying. How do you know God's opinion of you is always positive, always unchanging, and always satisfying?

It is the gospel. Because of the gospel, any Christian finds assurance by knowing God likes them and will always be for them (Romans 8:31–39). To be accepted by God, you have to accept the works of Jesus. God will never accept you based on your works (Ephesians 2:8–9).

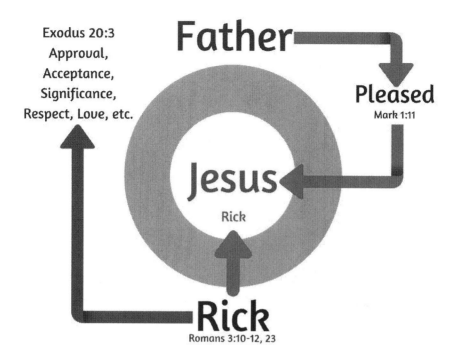

If you had to please God through your works, you would never please Him (Hebrews 11:6). Your inability to please God is one of the ironies regarding fear of man.

- You will never be able to please others entirely by your works.
- You will never be able to please God by your works.

The difference between the Lord and people is the Lord gives you another way to gain His approval. You can accept the works of His Son. People typically do not give you another option. You will always be a slave to those with whom you crave approval. What you did today to win someone's love will not be enough tomorrow or next week.

Seeking the approval of others is an endless, exhausting cycle. It is also breaking the first commandment (Exodus 20:3). The worship of other people's opinions is putting other gods between you and the true and living God. It is an idolatry that makes you a puppet to the vacillating opinion of the person you hope will like you.

Worshipping God is not that way. Winning His forever approval was finished through Christ (John 19:30). A way was opened up through Jesus after He lived, died, rose, and ascended to heaven. All a person has to do is get in the Son to be free. In the Son is the place to feel and experience the full pleasure of the Father. The only way to please God is by having faith in His Son. Get in Him and feel God's pleasure.

It is odd—though I do it, too—for a Christian to continue to strive for the approval of others when God is holding out the free blessing of full acceptance through Jesus. The Father poured out His wrath on His Son. Christ became the satisfying sacrifice for anyone who wants it. He took our place. All we have to do is believe. As Moses told the folks who were being attacked by the fiery serpents, "Look and live," that is all we have to do (Numbers 21:8; John 3:14).

Call to Action

1. Do you struggle with fear of others? Is there someone you would like to accept you?

2. Why are you that way? What has shaped you to fear others?

3. What do you want from them? Do you see how that craving has captured your mind?

4. Why does God not bring satisfaction to you? Why are you looking outside the fullness you have in Christ to find contentment through others?

5. Will you talk to someone about this struggle?

Chapter 11

Taking Thoughts Captive

Have you ever had someone accuse you of something that was not true? Have you ever accused yourself of something that was not true? Either way, whether from you or another person, any false argument launched against yourself can turn into a stronghold in your mind that could be spiritually debilitating.

"For the weapons of our warfare are not of the flesh but have divine power to destroy strongholds. We destroy arguments and every lofty opinion raised against the knowledge of God, and take every thought captive to obey Christ" (2 Corinthians 10:4–5).

You are susceptible to false arguments that can control your mind. These recurring thought patterns, when left unchecked, will become the dominating arguments of your mind, even to the point where they become your new truth—your new way of thinking.

A Case Study: Madison was such a person. Fear bound her. Some call it insecurity, which is an appropriate term. She was an insecure young woman, who was preoccupied with the arguments that swirled in her head. The controlling opinion of others was a stronghold that Madison seemingly could not break. Even though she knew God's opinion of her was perfect because of Christ, she could not live in the freedom of His empowering favor.

She had learned early in life how performing for others was the way to be accepted. Her daddy taught her this by his passive parenting style, and in the brief moments when he did say something, it was discouraging. Her childhood experiences helped to shape her as a people-pleaser. She was motivated not to disappoint others so she would not incur their displeasure. She became all things to all people with the hope of being accepted.

In time, she learned what others expected her to be. Though she was excited during her early years with Christ, eventually the old arguments of being disapproved came back. This stronghold was never successfully broken. She never learned how to take every thought captive. She learned how to be saved, but never learned how to mature in her sanctification. Her former manner of life, which was corrupt through deceptive desires for someone to like her, had a controlling influence in her mind.

"To put off your old self, which belongs to your former manner of life and is corrupt through deceitful desires, and to be renewed in the spirit of your minds" (Ephesians 4:22–23).

She continued to live the way she had always lived even though she was a believer. She had not learned how to renew her mind according to true right living and true holiness. She was what I call an unbelieving believer—a Christian who still lives according to an un-Christian quality of life (Mark 9:24).

"And to put on the new self, created after the likeness of God in true righteousness and holiness" (Ephesians 4:24).

A Spiritual Warfare

Madison was in warfare with her mind. She was under attack. According to Paul, this was more than just a human living in a human body while being attacked by the negativity of other people. Madison also lives in a spiritual world where there are real demonic forces who are out to destroy the knowledge of Christ that is resident in her.

94

The evil spiritual world cannot utterly destroy any Christian because Satan is not God's evil equal, but there are demonic forces that would enjoy nothing more than to derail a child of God from making His name great.

- Plan A for the devil is to keep all people from believing in Christ.
- Plan B for the devil is to keep all Christians from maturing in Christ.

Paul called what I am describing spiritual warfare in 2 Corinthians 10:3–6. He viewed his Christian life as a life of spiritual warfare. He knew where the primary battle came from and this knowledge served him well in his fight for his sanctification.

"For though we walk in the flesh, we are not waging war according to the flesh" (2 Corinthians 10:3).

Do you know you are in spiritual warfare? Do you know that there is a constant spiritual battle happening in this world and that you are part of it? You are not a sideline reporter but an active participant.

"And the LORD said to Satan, 'Behold, all that he has is in your hand. Only against him do not stretch out your hand.' So Satan went out from the presence of the LORD" (Job 1:12).

What Paul is teaching here is not new. Spiritual warfare has been going on since Adam and Eve took their first bite of disobedience. The Devil tried to knock them off, and he succeeded to a degree. He and his minions are trying to circumvent the work of God in your life too. Do you know that you have weapons to fight these spiritual battles—weapons that are divinely empowered? Do you know that God designed these weapons with the power to destroy the strongholds in your mind?

Madison did not know this. One of the tricks of the evil one is to disorient and deceive. Deception is what Satan did to Eve, which is what was happening to Madison. She, like her predecessor, had bought the lie. She had learned to believe that there is something wrong with her. Owning her faith and living as a new creation in Christ were helpful theological ideas that had a limited effect in her life. She was so wrapped up in her fear that she did not know how to live in the freedom that God's gospel provides.

What Is a Stronghold?

The forces that are against you in the spirit world are no different from the forces that are against you in the physical world, in that they both desire the same thing: to take your mind captive. The real question is how you are going to respond and fight against the forces that are against you, regardless of what constitutes these forces.

You have the power resident within you to fight against the strongholds that seek to take your mind captive. These weapons of warfare are the divinely empowered truths of the gospel. The real question is whether you will use these weapons to destroy the strongholds—the arguments and arrogant opinions that are raised up against God's revealed truth.

Stronghold Defined: A stronghold is a mental argument you believe that contradicts the person and power of Christ. A stronghold is a thought fortress of arguments designed to take your mind captive and hold you prisoner. These fortresses are designed to negate the person of Christ and His power (the gospel) in your life.

Madison had bought the lie of insecurity or fear of others (Proverbs 29:25). Her fear ensnared her to a life of bondage, as manifested through people-pleasing, peer pressure, worry and anxiety. She was overly concerned about what others thought about her. She was hyper-focused about nearly everything regarding herself.

She second-guessed her thoughts, questions, and comments. She doubted her choices and actions. She anxiously controlled how she looked in public and what she wore. Satanic forces could not destroy her soul (Plan A), but they could influence her mind until her usefulness in making God's name great was marginalized (Plan B). Taking every evil argument captive and making it bow to the name of Jesus was an illusionary, theological pipe dream.

Strongholds in Your Head?

God is the truth, and His purpose for coming to this world was to transform you so that you could walk in His truth. The Devil's job is to disrupt the truth God provides by motivating you to believe a lie. He hopes to set up deceitful strongholds in your mind.

"I have no greater joy than to hear that my children are walking in the truth" (3 John 1:4).

"When the Spirit of truth comes, he will guide you into all the truth" (John 16:13a).

"Sanctify them in the truth; your word is truth" (John 17:17).

What lies keep the gospel from dominating your thought life? What strongholds have been set up in your mind that hinder the sanctifying work of God in your life? What sinful thought fortresses reside in your head?

- Lies You Tell Yourself – I have to be perfect. I must be happy. I need people to agree with me. I cannot shake my past. I deserve better than this.
- Lies the World Tells You – I must be true to myself. I am number one. I am only human; everybody makes mistakes.

- Lies You Say in Your Marriage – It is your fault. If I had not married you. You make me so mad. Why cannot you be like so and so? I wish I were like so and so.
- Lies That Distort the Gospel – I must earn God's love. God will not protect me. God does not love me. I can do what I want, and God will forgive me. If I were more spiritual, I would not struggle like this. God will bless me if I obey.
- Lies from the Questions We Ask – Does God really hear me? Does God really love me? Has God abandoned me? Why does God not stop the pain?

When these types of thought-fortress-lies continue to roll around in your head, they will take your mind captive and will move you out of line with the gospel (Galatians 2:14). Outside gospel lines will ultimately reduce Jesus to become less than what He should be and the Spirit's power in your life will be reduced to less than what it can be.

Fighting the Fight with God's Truth

It is essential that you arm yourself with God's truth to overcome these strongholds—these thought fortresses. You cannot arm yourself with fleshly weapons. If you do, you may feel as though you have won the battle, but it will be more lies heaped upon the original lies. Fleshly weapons come from your human strength. The table provides a few of the commonly used weapons to fight the lies listed in the above section.

Adultery	Porn	Alcohol	Anger
Medication	Shopping	Unforgiveness	Bitterness
Gossip	Worry	Self-righteous	Anxiety
Exercise	Money	Education	Competition

There are plenty more. You will notice how not all of these things are necessarily bad. It is when you use them as the means to feel better about yourself or to pull yourself out of the dumps while not living in the freedom and the power the gospel provides.

Ultimately, these things will not work. They will further enslave you while creating more dysfunction in your relationships. Spiritual warfare looks different. Spiritual warfare contextualizes itself in the gospel—the person and work of Jesus Christ—on your behalf. He is the one you need to cooperate with in the battle for your mind.

I am going to take each lie noted above and pull it through a gospel filter. I am going to lay the gospel hammer on it to crush its head (Genesis 3:15), which I hope will be the beginning of your personal journaling to take your thoughts captive.

- Lies You Tell Yourself – I have to be perfect.

You do not have to be perfect. In fact, if you try to be perfect, you will be rejecting the righteousness of Christ, while choosing to hold up your righteousness as the answer. Not accepting Christ's righteousness is another gospel—your gospel of self-atonement. Not admitting the truth of your imperfection makes you a liar (1 John 1:8).

- Lies the World Tells You – You must be true to yourself.

You must be faithful to Christ. He is the one you live for, not for yourself. Living for yourself is the lie of the world—a self-centered, anti-Christ way of thinking. You are to die to yourself while fully trusting Christ who knows better than you do.

- Lies You Say in Your Marriage – It is your fault. I deserve better.

You will never be happy if things always go your way. You will implode through your frequent imbibing of self-centeredness. You are called to be content as you learn how to be sufficient through Christ rather than your personal preferences or what may even be good desires (Philippians 4:11–13).

- Lies That Distort the Gospel – I must earn God's love. God won't protect me.

Jesus Christ died for you on the cross. He, who was in the form of God, took on the form of a servant to rescue you. There is no greater love than a man who will lay down his life for another person. (Read Philippians 2:5–11; Romans 5:6–9; John 15:13.)

- Lies from the Questions We Ask – Does God really hear me?

The answer is similar to what you just read in #4 while adding to this a correct understanding of a theology of suffering. You are called to suffer, but if you equate suffering to God distancing Himself, you will not be able to understand God the way you should (1 Peter 2:18–25).

Madison's battles were not primarily against the people in her world. Sure, her daddy did give her a raw deal. She also had some other bad things happen to her, which were caused by others. But her battles went much deeper than the things done to her. She was in a spiritual battle with the evil influences of this evil world.

When Satan tempted Christ, there would not have been a temptation if Satan could not deliver on what he was offering. Your temptations come when your desires are influenced by Satan, and the temptation is real because he can give you your evil desires.

When your desires cooperate with evil influences, you can rest assured a stronghold will be set up in your mind. When those lies take your brain captive, your body will follow suit. When you immerse your life mostly in the things of this world and its influences, you will be coerced, controlled, and captured by the things of this world, and that warfare will be in your mind.

A gospel-informed mind can quickly take renegade thoughts captive to obey Christ, but you must take the battle in you seriously because your enemy takes it seriously. You must be influenced more by the Spirit to desire the things of God. It is also essential that you surround yourself with people who can help you in this battle for your mind.

Call to Action

1. There are several questions throughout this chapter. Will you journal them before the Lord?

2. What lies do you believe?

3. Have they developed into strongholds?

4. What has been the fallout from such strongholds?

5. Will you enlist the help of others to help you destroy these strongholds?

Chapter 12

God Puts You to Death

Did you know God is working behind the scenes to undermine any remaining self-reliance in you so that you will be able to trust Him more effectively? Exhibit A for this kind of teaching is the Apostle Paul. He had a God-ordained difficult life. He endured many hardships.

Why?

Quite simply because he knew Christ. It is important for you to understand how knowing Christ does not give you the option to forego suffering (Luke 14:26–27). Knowing Christ ensures personal suffering.

To know Jesus is a call to die (Luke 9:23). For Paul, suffering was not a lifestyle to spurn but a means God used to push him to true greatness.

"For we were so utterly burdened beyond our strength that we despaired of life itself. Indeed, we felt that we had received the sentence of death. But that was to make us rely not on ourselves but on God" (2 Corinthians 1:8–9a).

Paul's understanding of the mysteries of suffering gives you a couple of serious questions to ponder: What animates your innermost thoughts? What drives your greatest desires?

1. Is it your amazement at knowing Christ and being known by Him?
2. Or is it your personal desire for a better kind of life than what you are currently living?

"That I may know him and the power of his resurrection, and may share his sufferings, becoming like him in his death" (Philippians 3:10).

"Truly, truly, I say to you, unless a grain of wheat falls into the earth and dies, it remains alone; but if it dies, it bears much fruit" (John 12:24).

"I have been crucified with Christ. It is no longer I who live, but Christ who lives in me. And the life I now live in the flesh I live by faith in the Son of God, who loved me and gave himself for me" (Galatians 2:20).

Knowing Christ and being able to tell others about Christ was the purpose of Paul's life. This singular animating passion did not coexist with a desire to overcome his problems. He knew better. He perceived the point of his problems, which were to enable him to put Christ on display more effectively.

Suffering in Paul's life was like a magnifying glass. It allowed him to magnify Christ to his sphere of influence (Psalm 34:3). Suffering is one of those mysteries God gives to us so that we can understand Him more clearly. Equipped with this kind of understanding, you will be enabled to enjoy a deeper life with Him. It is a maturity that does not make suffering disappear. It is the suffering that fuels and sustains Christlike maturity.

Celebrate Recovery?

One of the unintended consequences of the biblical counseling movement is that some people believe counseling is a means to make their problems go away. And some counselors succumb to this expectation by "feeling pressure" to help counselees resolve the problems in their lives according to how they want them fixed.

"Three times I pleaded with the Lord about this, that it should leave me. But he said to me, 'My grace is sufficient for you, for my power is made perfect in weakness'" (2 Corinthians 12:8–9a).

Imagine if the great apostle Paul came to you with a thorn in his flesh. Imagine also that you knew he was a deeply spiritual man who loved God with his whole heart and was doggedly determined to tell others about Christ. He was a mature Christian, not a nominal one.

Furthermore, he told you about his problem and how he had committed it to prayer, asking God to remove the thorn in his flesh. Now he has come to you because he wants your help to eliminate the thorn. Here is a key piece of information: God is not, will not, cannot, and should not remove this thorn from Paul's life. Paul will live the rest of his life with a thorn in his flesh. That is God's irrevocable will for your counselee, Paul.

"But he is unchangeable, and who can turn him back? What he desires, that he does. For he will complete what he appoints for me, and many such things are in his mind" (Job 23:13–14).

God did not write the Bible so that we can celebrate recovery. For Paul, he never recovered. The celebration you see in the Scriptures is a Savior who transforms you through the power of the gospel, which happens at times by not removing the thorns in your life. He did not come to give you a great marriage, disease-free body, and financial freedom.

Though there are present tense and earthly benefits to living godly while humbly applying the truths of the Word of God to your life, the problem-free priorities and expectations that most people in our culture consider a right are not promises.

Our culture is trying to figure out how to overcome through therapy. The God-centered Christian has found a better way, which comes through celebrating the transformation that shapes a person into the likeness of Jesus Christ. And so often this kind of change happens because of suffering.

The biblical realist knows he cannot escape suffering. The realist also knows that suffering and the good life are not always hostile to each other. Disciplers, pastors, and counselors must be clear on this matter. They must not make problem removal their number one goal. There are two reasons for this:

1. It could be that God wants you to keep your thorn stuck in your flesh because that is the best way for you to put His Son on display.

2. It could be that God wants you to get rid of your thorn in the flesh because that is the best way for you to put His Son on display.

Your primary goal should be to put Jesus on display in your life regardless of how God chooses to accomplish it. This idea leads to an all-important question: what do you want to define your life?

1. Are you more interested in putting God's name on display through your suffering?

2. Are you more interested in removing your suffering, regardless if it brings glory to God?

To Suffer or Not Is Not the Question

The promise of the therapeutic culture is to get rid of your problems. The promise of God is to find strength through your problems.

"Therefore I will boast all the more gladly of my weaknesses, so that the power of Christ may rest upon me. For the sake of Christ, then, I am content with weaknesses, insults, hardships, persecutions, and calamities. For when I am weak, then I am strong" (2 Corinthians 12:9b–10).

A beautiful relationship, a great job, and financial security are remarkable outcomes for anyone, but Christ did not come to give you those things. Jesus came to die on a cross so that you could have an example to follow. You must walk in His steps to find a better life.

"For to this you have been called, because Christ also suffered for you, leaving you an example, so that you might follow in his steps" (1 Peter 2:21).

When sin came into the world, violence, disease, and corruption came along with it. Every person became a bad person (Isaiah 64:6; Romans 3:10–12). And bad things happen to bad people. Christ did not come to die to change violence, disease, or corruption. He came to change lives.

Though the death and resurrection of the Savior have slowed down the onslaught of sin, it was not the point of the gospel. His point was to give you His life so that you could be in Him while looking forward to a better world to come (Hebrews 11:10). You find your strength, glory, hope, and praise in God rather than in a perfect relationship or a healthy body. It's a person's unwillingness to embrace this kind of theology of suffering that opens the door to discouragement and depression.

The longer it takes a person to find strength in suffering, the more susceptible they will be to discouragement. Our therapeutic culture is opposed to this kind of teaching because they are beholden to an anti-suffering message. Part of the American dream is to remove all suffering from everyone, which is untenable teaching that does not factor in the doctrine of fallenness.

If your goal is to rid yourself of your problems, but you cannot get to that utopian place, you may be set up for unresolvable disappointment. If medications do not work or if a divorce does not give you a better life, you will not be far from depression.

1. How influenced have you become by the "best life now" mantra of our culture?

2. How has the prosperity drumbeat of the world detracted you from the Christological purposes of your life?

You can measure how you think about these questions by examining how you respond to the difficult challenges that are in your life. If you have peace, hope, and rest in the midst of your deepest trials, you have not been ensnared by the culture's suffering-free promise.

God Is Looking for Weak People

If you're going to walk with God, it is not your strength that God is going to use. He can't. He won't. He will not compete with you. He puts His treasure in jars of clay (2 Corinthians 4:7). God works through weakness and brokenness, not personal might or high intellect (Zechariah 4:6). It is your weakness that will release His strength to be perfected in you.

If your primary purpose in life is to be healthy and wealthy, you will be working counter to the purposes of God, and your frustrations will mount. Resisting God's suffering-centric plans for you will send you into a black hole of hopelessness. The way up is most assuredly down. The gospel narrative always cuts against the grain of the world's narrative (1 Corinthians 1:25).

The counter-intuitive gospel does not mean being sick, poor, and having dysfunctional relationships are the only ways to be strengthened by God. The idea in view here is not celebrating sin or suffering but celebrating Christ regardless of your circumstances. The only way you can be strong is by living in God's strength, not your own. The only way you can actually overcome is by celebrating God's strength through your weakness, brokenness, sickness, and poverty.

Let me reiterate: I am not saying you should contract HIV to be strong. I'm not saying you should intentionally become bankrupt to unleash God's power in your life. I'm saying that your circumstances, whatever they are, become a means to find God's strength, hope, peace, and contentment.

It could be that God will choose to "raise you from negative circumstances," but, again, that cannot be your first or most important prayer request. Your first and greatest desire must be to die in Christ, which does unleash God's perfected power in your life (John 12:24).

The beginning of this process of embracing Christ's death as your soul-sustaining strength is prayer. Ask the Father to help you walk through the incremental, systematic, and purposeful death of Christ (Galatians 2:20). The Lord will help you die to yourself (Isaiah 53:10).

You will have to let go of your strength to hold on to His strength. Perhaps this sample prayer from the Valley of Vision prayer book may guide you in grasping some of these deeper truths.

The Valley of Vision

Lord, high and holy, meek and lowly, Thou hast brought me to the valley of vision, where I live in the depths but see Thee in the heights; hemmed in by mountains of sin I behold Thy glory. Let me learn by paradox that the way down is the way up, that to be low is to be high, that the broken heart is the healed heart, that the contrite spirit is the rejoicing spirit, that the repenting soul is the victorious soul, that to have nothing is to possess all, that to bear the cross is to wear the crown, that to give is to receive, that the valley is the place of vision. Lord, in the daytime stars can be seen from deepest wells, and the deeper the wells the brighter Thy stars shine; let me find Thy light in my darkness, Thy life in my death, Thy joy in my sorrow, Thy grace in my sin, Thy riches in my poverty, Thy glory in my valley.

Call to Action

1. Are you struggling?
2. Are you finding God's strength in your weakness? Perhaps this would be an excellent time to talk to someone about this.
3. Do you know why you are not able to find His perfected power in you?
4. Is there something you want more than Christ as your animating center?

5. I am not saying you have to lose that thing you want but are you willing to lose that thing if losing it is the only way to find peace and strength with God (Luke 22:42)?

Chapter 13

Beyond Your Ability?

My friend Shanna used to be part of the disappointed and discouraged crowd. She was an overworked, over-challenged, and overwhelmed single mom. She lived in a world where she never seemed to get on top of things.

Initially, her tenacious grit compelled her to try harder. She bought into the culture's worldview of independence and self-reliance. She determined never to lose and never give up. It was win-win at all costs and, no matter how difficult things became, her mantra was, "When things get tough, the tough get going." Her perspective worked well until her meltdowns outnumbered her victories.

Finally, her boss called her in and gave her an ultimatum—no more outbursts. She freaked. Rather than seeking God, she gave herself over to fear and worry, which eventually turned into bitterness and compounded anxiety. Then depression came calling. Shanna's internal turmoil put her between a rock and a hard place—to the point where she thought about suicide.

"But we have this treasure in jars of clay, to show that the surpassing power belongs to God and not to us" (2 Corinthians 4:7).

You're Not Supposed to Succeed

In a last-ditch effort to pull herself out of her funk, she considered counseling. After listening to her story of woe for nearly an hour, I said, "God is calling you to do what you cannot do with the ability you do not have." She gave me a quizzical look to which I followed with, "He wants it this way. What you're going through is the will of God for your life. God wants to bring you to a place where you cannot fix yourself or your life because His desire is for you to rely on Him."

"For we do not want you to be unaware, brothers, of the affliction we experienced in Asia. For we were so utterly burdened beyond our strength that we despaired of life itself. Indeed, we felt that we had received the sentence of death. But that was to make us rely not on ourselves but on God who raises the dead" (2 Corinthians 1:8–9).

A suffering-sending God was hard for her to hear initially. She was embarrassed about not being able to do it all by herself. Everything that could go wrong was going wrong, and she believed if it were not wrong now, it would be wrong shortly. She tried to keep up but just could not do it anymore.

- She had no husband.
- All her friends were stay-at-home moms.
- Her kids wore hand-me-downs.
- She could not afford family vacations.
- Her car was a clunker.
- She had to pull the children out of private school.
- Her ex-husband was an every-other-weekend unholy terror.

Her response to all of this was to internalize her problems, never utter a word, and redouble her efforts. Her plan was not working. Sometimes life is meant to go bad because it is the only way God can get our attention. He had Shanna's attention now. She was crying out for help.

A plea for help, out of a heart of genuine brokenness, is the prayer He was leading her to share with Him. Shanna had to come to the place where we all should come. Say this out loud, "I am not self-reliant."

You were not meant to win all the time. Sometimes God has to run you into a ditch to free you from yourself. The self-sufficient person does not need God. It is a deceptive and tempting approach to life that does not work. Paul was right:

"I can do all things through him who strengthens me" (Philippians 4:13).

Win-win Is a Worship Disorder

To say, "I can do all things through me who strengthens me" is a worship disorder of the worst kind. It is not God's intention to let us do things our way, according to our agenda, while working within our personal gifting and well-honed skill set (Genesis 11:6).

It can never be win-win all the time for all people with or without God. He is too merciful to allow this to happen to His fallen creation. He insists we do things according to His will while He receives glory for what He accomplishes through us (Romans 11:36; Philippians 2:12–13).

The implication is clear: there will be times when God will accomplish things outside of your abilities. It is important for you to understand this. You are to work under His power and His strength rather than your own. Part of the reason for this is because people are "glory hogs." Isn't it true that in your heart of hearts you love praise and adoration? I do. There is a desire within us to be like a god (Genesis 3:5), which is at the heart of our self-reliant, Adamic fallenness.

This kind of self-centered thinking puts you in competition with God, as well as with others. You demand your way. God requires His way. Guess who is going to win that tug-of-war? To help you get over yourself, the Lord mercifully puts you in a place or a situation where you cannot control or manipulate the outcome, which is what happened to Shanna. She was left with two choices:

113

1. She could stubbornly press on, to her compounded shame and other people's personal hurt.
2. She could relinquish her rights to her situation and trust God's way—even if it does not make sense.

Here are a few examples of times when God's way is hard to embrace. You decide. Read over these questions and honestly analyze yourself. Which is easier: to respond in your strength or to respond in God's strength?

1. When it's time to forgive someone who has hurt you?
2. When it's time to regularly submit to and serve your spouse (Ephesians 5:21)?
3. When it's time to ask forgiveness first?
4. When it's time to share your inner struggles to your small group or your friends?
5. When it's time to seek forgiveness from someone you believe has a worse sin than yours?

Did you know God is regularly testing you by giving you opportunities like these to trust Him? Typically, these moments happen when you do not want to trust Him, or you genuinely do not understand how to trust Him. In either case, He is asking you to do what you may not be willing to do or what you do not have the wisdom, insight, clarity, or knowledge to do.

God Works Beyond Your Ability

"But Jesus said, 'They need not go away; you give them something to eat.' They said to him, 'We have only five loaves here and two fish.' And he said, 'Bring them here to me.' Then he ordered the crowds to sit down on the grass, and taking the five loaves and the two fish, he looked up to heaven and said a

blessing. Then he broke the loaves and gave them to the disciples, and the disciples gave them to the crowds" (Matthew 14:16–19).

When the Lord came upon 5,000 people (not counting the women or the children) who were hungry and needing food, it was not within the disciple's ability to feed them.

1. At that moment, they were working outside of their collective strengths.

2. At that moment, Jesus had them right where He wanted them.

The perfect sweet spot with the Lord is when we have to trust Him rather than ourselves. We are called to walk by faith, not by our strength, cleverness, or insights. The disciples knew there was not enough bread and fish to feed 5,000 people. They were right. There was not enough provision to get the job done. Though they could not see past the bread in their baskets, Jesus could.

He stepped up and provided when their hands were empty. But the story gets better. Christ made what the disciples could not make, and He used the disciples to distribute what He provided. How kind of the Lord.

He provides what you cannot and chooses to use you in spite of your complaining and negativity. Can you imagine lodging a complaint against the Lord because you have assessed the situation and determined the job is too big, too hard, or too complicated? Then He comes through by doing the impossible.

There have been many instances in my life where I assessed the situation, as well as my abilities and resources to fix the situation, and promptly concluded the problems were too big or too complicated to repair. Then the Lord did the unexpected.

1. He provided.

2. He accomplished.

3. But He did not stop there.

Like the disciples in His day, He allowed me to be part of the process of helping those with whom I was previously lodging my complaints. God wants a relationship with me, but that relationship cannot be what it needs to be until I am willing to trust Him to do what I cannot do. I have to genuinely come to the end of myself (Luke 15:17).

Call to Action

1. Are you in a situation where there is seemingly no good way out of the mess?
2. Are you stuck?
3. Are you working outside your ability to pull off goals?

Working outside of your ability is not a bad thing. Sometimes it is the only right thing. It happens to me every day. Literally, I am confronted daily with people and situations that I cannot fix. Changing people is outside the scope of my responsibilities. It is a pay grade well above mine. When I began counseling, not being able to fix people kept me awake at night. Then I learned that if I could succeed in the people-fixing business, I would not need God.

The Lord kindly reminded me that there was a Savior and I was not Him. He helped me to repent of my self-reliant thinking while turning to Him for solutions. My job is much simpler than fixing people; I point them to Jesus. Like John the Baptist, I am a sign post. When people come to me for help, I point them to Christ. I have taken up John's mantra,

"He must increase and I must decrease" (John 3:30).

Let the Gospel Speak to Your Self-Reliance

When you come to the place where it does not make sense, or you cannot figure it out, may I make a suggestion? How about if you recalibrate your

116

thinking around the gospel? There is nothing like the gospel narrative to bring clarity to our challenges.

Imagine standing at the foot of Golgotha on the day they crucified the Savior. The disciples were there—the same friends who appealed to Christ to take over the Roman world. There they stood watching their friend die at the hands of the Romans. It was all backward to them. It seemed so wrong that He would die.

1. Has your life ever seemed backward—going the wrong way?
2. Has it ever seemed as though it was heading in a different place from what you expected?

That is what the disciples felt on the day their friend died. Watching Christ die pushed them outside the bounds of their human understanding. They wanted, expected, and demanded a king. The most likely candidate to succeed was now bleeding and dying on a cruel cross. They were baffled. Only a few hours earlier, Peter had his sword drawn and was ready to carve up a victory for Jesus.

Now he is looking at King Jesus bleeding to death. They were confused, hopeless, angry, and in despair as they saw all their dreams dying on a cross. That story is no different from your story in that God is always up to something better than what you can perceive. It appeared the Romans murdered the Savior, but actually, His Father executed Him (Isaiah 53:10). Why? Because being a king 2,000 years ago was not nearly as good as being a King in eternity.

Initially, the disciples did not perceive this. Can you look back on your life and thank the Lord that He did not give you the desires of your heart in a time when you were asking for something? I am glad that He did not give the disciples their wishes.

Will You Walk by Faith?

Unfortunately, we are uncomfortable not being in the know. We do not like living by faith (Romans 14:23). We want to know outcomes before we begin. We want to know it will be okay before we move forward.

We want to work within our abilities rather than the Lord's strength. We are no different from the disciples. God is calling you to trust Him—to walk by faith (Matthew 14:31). He will not give you all the answers you desire. If He did, you would be back to trusting yourself again. He is calling you to stop trusting yourself. Nothing will bring clarity to this faith tension like the gospel story.

That story needs to inform your thinking, rather than your wits. Whose story are you living? The disciples wanted to live for their story. God had another story in mind. Even when you do not understand what God is doing in your life, it is humble and wise to thank Him with expressions of gratitude for His leadership in your life. Your gratitude does not mean your life will change a lot or at all.

Shanna's life did not change, but her thoughts about God did. As she persistently preached the gospel narrative to herself, she experienced a calm soul. Through her ordeal, like the disciples, God brought her to an end of herself. Even though she did not exactly know what He was up to, she decided to trust Him, albeit imperfectly.

If God is holding back from you what you desire, I appeal to you to consider the possibility that He has something better for you. Though He may not give you what you want at the moment, whatever He has planned for you will be far better than you could ever imagine (Ephesians 3:20).

The best way to begin this kind of reorientation of the mind is to express gratitude to Him for His sovereign care in your life. Giving thanks is the will of God for you (1 Thessalonians 5:18). Begin right now. Make it your moment-by-moment habit. Perhaps keeping a daily list of things you are thankful for would be a good start.

Chapter 14

Overcoming Self-Reliance

The self-reliant person lives in a fantasy world. It is not a real world because it is an impossible feat to achieve. Nobody can be self-sufficient. Not even Jesus had that ability. He grew physically (Luke 2:40, 52). He was tired (John 4:6) and became thirsty (John 19:28). He hungered (Matthew 4:2) and experienced physical weakness (Matthew 4:11; Luke 23:26). And He died (Luke 23:46).

To pursue a self-reliant lifestyle is to push yourself past the boundaries that Jesus would not dare to go (Luke 22:42). He resisted this temptation by choosing to do something that is counter-intuitive to self-sufficiency: He humbled Himself to the will of God (John 6:38).

"Though he was in the form of God, . . . [He] emptied himself, by taking the form of a servant, being born in the likeness of men. And being found in human form, he humbled himself by becoming obedient to the point of death, even death on a cross" (Philippians 2:6–8).

Self-sufficiency is the self-deceiving and isolating process of trying to be stronger and stronger while resisting the help of other people, especially help from the Lord. It is a sinful desire to build a lifestyle and reputation that releases a person from trusting God. Christ resisted this lifestyle choice.

He set aside His glorious reputation and powerful position with the Father to become a dependent human being. He embraced weakness so that He could tap into the strength of God (Luke 22:42; John 6:38).

Though self-reliance and God-reliance are similar in that they promote a person, there is an eternal difference between them. The God-reliant person desires to make God's name great. The self-reliant person craves to make his name great (Daniel 4:30; James 1:14–15).

Gospel Irony

The self-sufficient person presents the oddest of ironies. While his self-reliance projects the image of being strong and in control, the reality is he is weak and not in control. Like all humanity, he stands in need of God's empowering grace.

Self-reliance is smoke and mirrors. It is a sham. It's a form of insanity to pretend to be something you are not. You, like me, are broken and depraved (Romans 3:23). You are unable and incapable of successfully accomplishing and sustaining anything outside of God's proactive intervention and provision (1 Corinthians 4:7; Ephesians 2:1–9).

You are God-dependent whether you want to admit it or not. The people in the world are clamoring to promote themselves while trying to prove to anyone who will listen how they have it all together because they have tapped into their true selves and achieved their definition of greatness.

While they may want to impress or give the appearance of being impressive, they are hopeless and bankrupt, frantically resisting humanity's collective death march (Genesis 2:16–17). Real success has never been through self-effort, self-esteem, or self-reliance—three lifestyles that lead to competitive individualism.

"The sacrifices of God are a broken spirit; a broken and contrite heart, O God, you will not despise" (Psalm 51:17).

True success begins with a broken and humble posture before the Lord. You find the most profound picture of this gospel irony in the cross of Christ. His death on Adam's tree was God's strength and wisdom profoundly put on display.

"For the word of the cross is folly to those who are perishing, but to us who are being saved it is the power of God" (1 Corinthians 1:18).

Personal success is not through might and power (Zechariah 4:6). It is through weakness, as displayed by the humble heart who is willing to submit to God moment by moment, especially when life does not make sense (2 Corinthians 4:7 and 12:10).

Two Masters?

The nature and expectation of self-reliance are to reject God. It is a choice as to whether you want to serve yourself or serve the Lord. You cannot trust God and yourself at the same time. Though Jesus was talking to the Pharisees about money, He laid out a universal truth about the impossibility of simultaneously serving God and man when he said,

"No servant can serve two masters, for either he will hate the one and love the other, or he will be devoted to the one and despise the other. You cannot serve God and money" (Luke 16:13).

Because the temptation to be self-reliant is every person's temptation and struggle, I developed a mind map on the next page to help you gain a better perspective of the challenges and the solution regarding your struggle with God.

Breaking Down the Self-Reliant Person

Self-reliance is a dysfunction of the heart that speaks specifically to how you relate to God. You are called to believe God. In the mind map, I used synonyms like belief, hope, confidence, trust, and faith.

These words convey the idea of trusting the Lord. I am not using the word "trust" or "belief" in a salvific sense, meaning a lack of salvation if you

123

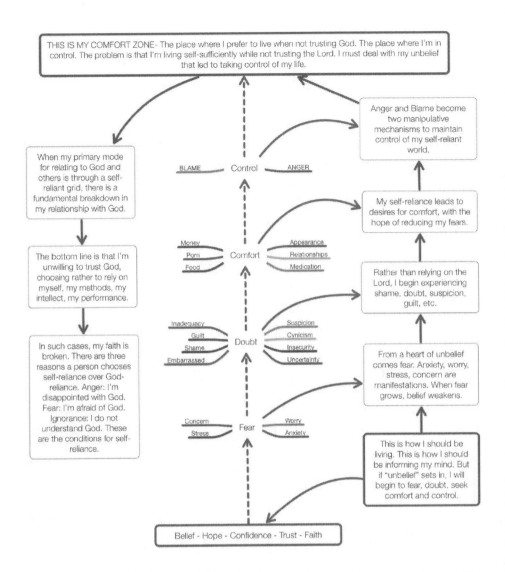

struggle with self-reliance. This sin is not the exclusive domain of the unbeliever. Anyone can be an occasional functional atheist even though they are born again.

Unbelieving Believer

"Immediately the father of the child cried out and said, 'I believe; help my unbelief!'" (Mark 9:24b)

Because it is not possible to perfectly trust God, you need to believe and re-believe over and over again. You must guard your heart daily while contextualized in a community that encourages and challenges your faith (Hebrews 10:24). If you do not place yourself in this kind of community, fear will begin to rule your heart.

When Adam chose to un-believe in the garden of Eden, he immediately began to fear. If you are not going to trust God fully, you will trust someone or something else. The most common and logical option for you to trust is yourself.

But you intuitively know you are not trustworthy. There is always an element of fear when you rely on yourself. Self-suspicion is what Adam experienced when he chose to depend on himself (Genesis 3:8–10). Note the progression in the mind map from a heart of trust to a heart of fear.

Most "pretending-to-be-strong people" have a hard time admitting their fears (2 Corinthians 1:8–9, 4:7, and 12:7–10). Their self-reliant worldview disdains and dismisses fear. They cannot make this accommodation for what they consider to be an aberration of the psyche. Admitting fear goes against their carefully crafted self-reliant image.

The word fear on the map represents the self-reliant person's heart. You could draw a heart around the word. Also, note the tributaries of fear—its spiritual feeders. I have placed four in this map: worry, anxiety, stress, and concern. You must feed fear for it to survive, and these four feeders keep fear alive and functioning in the self-reliant heart. The longer fear stays active in the heart, the more the person will be prone to doubt. Doubt is the natural outworking of fear.

This fear-to-doubt construct works out in the self-reliant person's behaviors. For example, he will become afraid or anxious about certain outcomes. Rather than trusting God, he will default to a habituated self-reliant mode to regain control of the situation. One of the most common "modes" to restore order to his self-controlled, self-perpetuated universe is anger. Anger is a manipulative tactic of the fearful person to regain control of what he believes he's losing.

In these anxious moments, he is not sure God will come through for him, so he takes matters into his hands. Though fear and self-reliance appear to be antithetical, as you can see, they are actually in cahoots. Self-reliance does a good job of masking a heart of fear.

Hiding Fear

There are many ways a person will mask fears, doubts, and insecurities. In the mind map, you will see the word comfort and the ancillary tributaries that feed the desire for comfort, like appearance, money, and anger.

Being god is hard. Self-reliance is exhausting work, which is why the self-reliant person has to find rest from running his universe. He does this by seeking means of comfort—a respite from self-centered, kingdom-building work. His go-to comfort cravings depend on the kind of person he is and how he enjoys sin (Hebrews 11:25). Here are a few examples:

Reputation – He finds comfort building his reputation. His self-made greatness feels good. It brings comfort. He can go to nearly inexhaustible lengths to maintain and promote his "I am in control—I am somebody" image.

Pornography – He finds comfort through women, whether on the net, his spouse, or someone else. The porn addict creates a theater for the mind, where his women are under his spell. Whenever he needs a "self-important booster shot," he can turn to his woman of choice to feed his ego.

Anger – He finds comfort by keeping his world in tightfisted control through the mechanism of anger. He uses anger either passively or aggressively as a manipulative tactic to stay in charge.

Anger caveat – He rarely chooses anger outside of a few close friends because he wants to maintain his reputation to the world at large. In most cases, only his wife, family, and a few associations will see his anger.

Comfort Zone

Because he is not God and cannot rule his universe like God, he has to whittle his world down to something more manageable—something he can control and perpetuate. This smallish universe is his comfort zone. You see it at the top of the mind map.

His comfort zone is the place where he enjoys what he has created. He is in control as long as he can keep his life contained in his hermetically sealed universe. Of course, the problem with this worldview is that life is not that neat, contained, or manageable. Life was not meant to be controlled by our self-effort.

You are called to live by faith in the Lord, not to live by faith in yourself and your abilities (Hebrews 11:6). You will quickly discern if you struggle with self-reliance by how you respond when life moves out of your comfort zone. You will be forced to make a decision either to trust God or try to regain control of your world according to your preferences.

Your responses to life situations will reveal the real motivations of your heart (Luke 6:45). The self-reliant person will not humble himself to God. He will not experience the greater work the Lord could do in his life. His primary objective will be to exercise whatever means necessary to regain control of his life.

His determination to be self-reliant makes it hard for him to trust others. He struggles to perceive there could be another way of doing things. His native response is to demand, manipulate, and engineer his way through the difficulty. He has an "I can do all things through me who strengthens me" mentality to get his way (Philippians 4:13).

If he does not repent of his self-reliance, he will alienate himself from his friends. Self-reliance does not build community. It promotes individualism. It does not create unity. It divides people, hurts feelings, creates misunderstandings, and instills relational dysfunction.

Call to Action

Self-reliance is a crisis of faith. You cure it by coming back to the gospel. If you are prone to rely on yourself, you must relearn how to re-believe.

1. What is a circumstance that tempts you to rely on yourself?
2. What do you think is motivating you to take matters into your hands?
3. Can you articulate why you are this way?

Self-reliance is a loud and proud declaration that God is not sufficient to take care of your life. You may be a believer in that you have been born a second time (John 3:7), but you are not entirely trusting the Lord in your sanctification. Here are a few questions that will assist you in thinking about why you are this way.

1. What is it about God that tempts you to not rely on Him?
2. Are you afraid of Him?
3. Are you angry at Him?
4. Are you unaware of how God can do more through your weakness than through your strengths?

The solution is to restore this gospel-dysfunction of the heart. It will not auto-correct. You must explore and repair what is broken. Your first call to action is to find a friend who will walk with you through this journey. With whom will you share this chapter?

Chapter 15

Four Steps to Change

Dad, why do you counsel someone so long? —Daughter

*I counsel for a long time because it takes a while to help someone change.
—Rick*

*It seems to me that it would only take a minute. You say, "Repent;" the
person changes and that is all you have to do. What else do you talk about with
them?—Daughter*

And we smile, though my daughter does have a point, which can cause one
to wonder how much relational conflict and dysfunction could we eliminate if
we followed her simply stated approach. I'm sure it wouldn't clean up all our
messes, but it would probably make quite a dent in some of the junk we spread
amongst our relationships.

Life Plan for Christian Maturity

Because repentance is not native to us, God is patient as He comes
alongside us to teach us how to change. After Adam first sinned, he decided not
to repent, choosing to place his problems on someone else (Genesis 3:12).

Ever tried that? As sons and daughters of Adam, blaming, rationalizing, or
justifying problems away are the things that tempt us as we adjust our fig
leaves (Genesis 3:7). Mercifully, God perseveres with us by not allowing us to
stay tangled in our sinful tendencies (Galatians 6:1). One of the primary means
of grace He uses to help us change is His Word. For example, when Paul was

129

teaching the young Pastor Timothy, he highlighted how God uses His Word to change us. Notice what He said:

"All Scripture is breathed out by God and profitable for teaching, for reproof, for correction, and for training in righteousness, that the man of God may be complete, equipped for every good work" (2 Timothy 3:16–17).

Four Elements to Change

Though this passage is often used to highlight and elevate God's inspired-sufficient-plenary-authoritative Word, which is good and right, I want to turn the passage over again and look at it in a more practical way. I'm going to highlight the four elements of change Paul lays out for you, and if consistently applied to your life, they will radically change you and your relationships.

After God had regenerated you, He began to teach you His Word—a process of recurring illumination, instruction, conviction, and transformation, which is called progressive sanctification. God's Word is one of the primary means for you to mature into Christlikeness. Through contexts and people, the Word of God penetrates your heart for the purpose of personal transformation.

"Sanctify them in the truth; your word is truth" (John 17:17).

If you follow Paul's prescriptive progression in this passage, you will notice how the use of God's Word is to stop dangerous thinking by reorienting your mind around sound teaching. The way the Lord terminates bad teaching—as noted in the Timothy template—is to rebuke you. The word rebuke means to knock down. The idea in view here is the Lord bringing sound teaching into your life to put you on your backside. Through the Spirit's illuminating conviction, you begin to see the light (1 John 1:7–10). How many times has God brought His Word to you to stop you from your course of action? Though sometimes God's adjustments in your life can be inconvenient and even painful, it is His mercy to care so much about you. He wants to change your life.

Before I proceed, take some time to assess yourself to see how well you are responding to Paul's first two points regarding the change process. The Word of God is profitable for teaching and rebuking. Here are some helpful questions for you and your friends to discuss regarding your teachableness and receptivity to rebuke.

Teaching

1. Are you teachable? (Are you easy to teach?)
2. Is it easy for people to care for you because of your hunger to be taught?
3. Do you seek to be taught by those you trust and those competent enough to teach you?
4. Are you a question asker? Do you pursue others with questions about how to change your life?
5. Does your guardedness about your reputation hinder others from speaking into your life?
6. Are you oversensitive? Does your insecurity hinder people from speaking into your life?

Because teaching is the door through which you will grow, it is incumbent upon you to be teachable. You will not be able to change your life if you are not teachable, the first step in the change process. Your teachability is the litmus test that will inform others about your seriousness to grow in Christ.

Rebuking

1. Can you be rebuked? Can you receive the corrective observations of others?

2. When someone reproves you, how do you initially respond?

3. When reproved, are you more focused on the person who said it and how they said it or on how you can humbly respond to what was said?

4. Do you pursue the reproving care of your friends?

5. Are you tempted to sulk or go into self-pity mode after someone reproves you?

6. Do you express gratitude to those who love you enough to bring correction into your life?

Being reproved or rebuked is tough stuff. Nobody enjoys it. To be willing to have others speak into your life is one of the high marks of Christian maturity. Rebuke-able people typically have humble and wise perspectives about themselves. They are rebuke-able because the gospel rightly informs them. (See Romans 3:10–12, 23, 5:12; Isaiah 64:6; 1 Timothy 1:15.)

Being informed by the gospel means you were in a helpless and worthless condition before the Lord chose to save you. You were dead in your sins, hell-bound, and outside of God's grace (Ephesians 2:1–10). Alienated from the life that is in God was your spiritual condition (Ephesians 4:18). Outside of God's favor was the Lord's view of you before salvation.

There is nothing anyone could say to you that is worse than what the Lord has previously declared about you. Understanding this aspect of the gospel releases you from the fear of what others can say about or do to you.

Couple this gospel truth of what you were to whom you are in Christ, then most assuredly you have nothing to protect or nothing to hide (Romans 8:31–39). If you have been born again (John 3:7; Romans 10:9, 13), you are a child of the King—a person who has gone from the worst possible position that you could be to the best possible place you will ever enjoy.

If you are not living daily in this gospel truth, temptations will lure you toward insecurity that will motivate you to protect and defend your reputation before others. That kind of pride will truncate the effectiveness in which your friends can speak into your life—a soul-stunting posture before the Lord and others.

Bad News Precedes Good News

While the gospel is the good news, its message implies there is bad news. If there were no bad news, you would not need the good news. The same is true in Paul's progressive keys to Christian maturity that he laid out for his friend Timothy.

Teaching brings reproof, which is supposed to knock you off your feet. That is the bad news. Thankfully, the Spirit of God would never leave you down and out (Psalm 23:3). He is the Healer who binds our wounds (Psalm 147:3). A careful and accurate rebuke from the Lord paves the way for His corrective measures that you can implement into your life. The word "corrected" means to be stood up or made erect.

It's important for you to know the Lord wants to correct you. God is a fixer. He does not rebuke you because He enjoys bringing pain into your life. There is always a redemptive purpose to His corrections. If the Lord does not convince you of this, you will be tentative about receiving His reproof (Hebrews 12:6).

Some will argue how they don't mind being rebuked by God, but it is the rebuke of sinful people that rubs them the wrong way. Horizontal soul care is a problem for sure. It would be great if people rebuked perfectly all the time, but that is not possible among fallen people. Imperfect people reproving imperfect people will have an element of imperfection in it.

Though there is a lot to say about wrongful rebukes, the point of this chapter is whether you are mature enough and hungry enough to find the Lord's rebuke even through imperfect vessels. Can you learn anything from a poorly given rebuke? You can if your goal is Christian maturity. Maybe later you can help the person who admonished you poorly.

Correction

1. Are you more likely to focus on the reproof or the correction? (The former is a tendency to be proud, while the latter is a tendency to be humble.)

2. Are you more preoccupied with arguing with the "rebuker" or with maturing in your sanctification for God's glory?

3. Do you believe you need others to help you walk through sanctification issues?

4. Do you enlist the help of your friends so you can change?

5. Do you believe others need you so you can help them walk through their sanctification issues?

6. Would you say your commitment to change is greater than your commitment to your reputation?

Christian Growth Here We Come

Paul's four progressive and essential keys to change are:

1. Teaching – "I want God's Word to teach me."

2. Reproving – "As I learn from God's Word, I expect it to reprove me on occasion."

3. Correcting – "To be reproved is a door that leads to correction."

4. Training – "After I'm corrected, I jump on God's training track where I'm able to run my race more effectively." (See Hebrews 12:1 and 1 Corinthians 9:24–27.)

Each time you make it through steps one, two, and three, you will be ready to participate in ongoing training for right living. This process of progressive sanctification is not a one-and-done deal. These steps are recurring and unending until you see Jesus.

Each day is a new opportunity to learn (teaching), fall (rebuke), get up (correction), and run a new way (training in righteousness). Imagine what it would be like if the Lord loved you enough to identify areas that could change your life regularly. That kind of love invigorates the soul. Only Christians possess that kind of incremental, ongoing, unending, progressive path to freedom in Christ. Only Christians can change in long-term and sustainable ways.

Imagine if the Lord saved you and left you to your former manner of life (Ephesians 4:22) with no way of changing—no chance to mature spiritually.

1. Teaching – How often do you learn something from God's Word?
2. Rebuke – How often do you let the free conviction from the Spirit course through your mind?
3. Correction – How often do you benefit from His rerouting correctives?
4. Training – How often have you taken a new path to run your race for the Lord?

"He restores my soul. He leads me in paths of righteousness for his name's sake" (Psalm 23:3).

Watch Out for Traps

To mature in this kind of progressive process, I recommend that you teach this to your family and friends. Invite them into your life growth plan. Appeal to them to come alongside you so you all can benefit from mutual and reciprocal gospel-shaped care. And, by all means, watch out for traps.

Trap #1 – Bad Experience – Many Christians have had bad experiences with other Christians. In such cases, they are tempted to map their bad experience over what God could be doing redemptively in their lives.

135

Sometimes your experience can be your worst enemy. It can also make you cynical about future grace, always thinking the worst about people's motives. Don't do that. Have faith in God (Hebrews 11:6). Let your faith in the current process that God has for you overcome the past evil that someone did to you. God's grace can outmaneuver and defeat your bad experiences regardless of what has happened to you.

Trap #2 – Isolation – Don't cut yourself off from a community. It is rare for a person to deteriorate in grace if they actively pursue a gospel-shaped community—a context that is loving and intentional in the personal and practical exploration of life change among friends.

Most of the time when I get in trouble is when I am isolating myself from the community. Sitting, soaking, and spectating on Sundays will not help you. You must engage God and others to change your life. Be open. Be honest. Be taught. Expect to be reproved. Look forward to correction. Run a spiritually productive race.

Call to Action

Your call to action is to work through the questions under the four headings in this chapter. Ready? Start running.

"Let us also lay aside every weight, and sin which clings so closely, and let us run with endurance the race that is set before us, looking to Jesus, the founder and perfecter of our faith, who for the joy that was set before him endured the cross, despising the shame, and is seated at the right hand of the throne of God" (Hebrews 12:1–2).

Chapter 16

You Must Know These

One of the more surprising things I have learned from a career in counseling is the average Christian does not know how to change. The Bible word for change is repentance.

The irony is that the purpose for Jesus's coming was so that we could change. The point and force of the gospel are about change. One of the reasons we have lost our way is because we think about change primarily from a salvation perspective rather than from a sanctification perspective.

The point of salvation is to get you into a position to change. The real change happens after you are born again. Like your physical birth, you were not complete when you came into the world, but only after years of growing into a fuller version of yourself were you mature (1 Peter 2:2). This process to maturity was what Paul was teaching the Ephesians.

"[You are] to put off your old self, which belongs to your former manner of life and is corrupt through deceitful desires, and to be renewed in the spirit of your minds, and to put on the new self, created after the likeness of God in true righteousness and holiness" (Ephesians 4:22–24).

Getting saved is not all you need. It is all you need to be justified and adopted and to secure your seat in heaven, but salvation does not change you in the way you need to be up-fitted for living in a fallen world. Paul was talking to saved people who needed to change. Their big problem was not being born again but working out their salvation (Philippians 2:12–13) in such a way that they could resolve their personal and relational problems. After laying the salvation foundation, you begin to build the house.

137

This is where too many Christian drop the ball. They simply do not know how to build the house. Then they marry people who do not know how to change. Then they have children who do not know how to change. The accumulative effect is ongoing exported dysfunction.

Let's make it personal: If someone came to you and asked you to unpack the doctrine of repentance, could you do it? Could you walk them through all the elements of change? There are thirteen elements in the process of change. Apart from being born again, learning and applying these things are the most important things you will ever do. The reason is because your life is made up of three parts:

1. You were lost.

2. You were saved.

3. You spend the rest of your life being sanctified.

If you have been saved, you are a stage three Christian. The rest of your life is about repentance—the ongoing process of changing or what is called progressive sanctification. You do not need to be born again, again, but you must always be evolving into Christlikeness.

The Sin Removing Process

Step One – Sin

Sin is the only negative in the process of change, and it is the reason for repentance. If sin did not happen, you would not need to repent, and Jesus would not have needed to come and die for you. Sin is the great separator that comes between you, God, and others.

The key to step one is having clear and theological sin categories. Without being tenacious and discerning regarding the identification of sin, you will never repent. The temptation for us is to soften sin by blaming it, justifying it, or rationalizing it away as though it doesn't exist.

These three anti-gospel approaches to sin will dull your life (Hebrews 5:12–14), quench the Spirit (1 Thessalonians 5:19), and keep you separated from the richness of the relationships that you could enjoy with God and others.

Let's take the "sin softening" test: using the sin of anger, see how well you are at identifying it in your life. From *The Anger Spectrum*, pick out the ways this sin manifests in your life. Without clear sin categories, you will never be able to change.

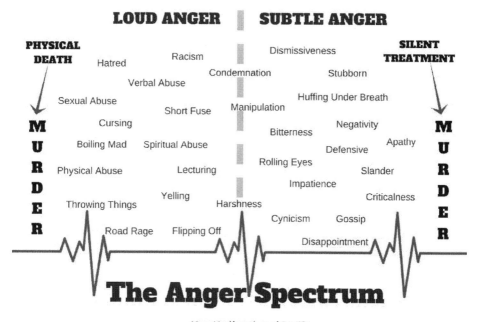

The Anger Spectrum

Many Manifestations of One Sin

Step Two – Guilt

When you sin, you are guilty before God. This is a nonnegotiable truth regardless of the awareness levels of sin in your life. God is the final authority, so when sin happens, there is guilt. Blaming, justifying, or rationalizing your sin away does not remove your guilt.

Though you can manipulate others or pretend your actions don't matter, God cannot be manipulated. Negotiating with sin will send your soul to a dark place. You do not want to be detached from God's perspective about your actions (Hebrews 3:7). To deny your sin is a form of insanity.

Step Three – Conviction

Conviction is a mercy from the Lord. It is the realization that you have done something wrong. At this point, you should respond to His mercy. Some people do not respond, and this is where their consciences begin to harden (1 Timothy 4:2; Romans 2:14–15).

In time, it becomes more difficult for them to sense when they have done wrong (Hebrews 4:7–8). If this happens, they will never be able to have their sin neutralized, which will be the death knell to their souls and relationships.

Step Four – Confession

Biff gets mad with Mable. He huffs under his breath after she does not respond promptly to him. Because Biff has solid sin categories, he immediately feels conviction from the Spirit of God, and he confesses his sin.

The word confess means to agree. Biff agrees with God that his huffing was a form of murder, according to James 4:1–2. His sensitivity to the Spirit moves him to make it clear with God and Mable that he understands what he did was sinful. He confesses his sin to both God and Mable.

The key to confession is for the sphere of the offense and the sphere of confession to be the same. Meaning, you should confess your sin to all the people who experienced your sin.

That is what Biff did.

Step Five – Pre-forgiveness

Typically, the need for repentance involves other people besides God. In the case of Biff, his wife was sinned against. This is where it gets dicey between people and where relationships become difficult because Mable must forgive Biff; he needs for her to release him from his sin.

But there is a problem: this is not the first time Biff sinned against Mable that way, which has been the impetus for her to harbor her own form of anger toward Biff. Mable is bitter. Though Biff is asking, she is unwilling to forgive him. This idea is called pre-forgiveness, a word I manufactured as a way of communicating the heart of Joseph before his brothers came to him to ask forgiveness (Genesis 50:20).

This was also the spirit of Christ when you came asking for His forgiveness. Being ready and willing to forgive the sinner is essential if you want to reconcile. If you have not done the preparatory work in your heart to forgive someone, when they do ask for forgiveness, you will have a hard time forgiving them.

Step Six – Forgiveness

Sin is not a one-way street. It takes two—the offender and the offended. If the victim is mature, there will be a willingness to grant forgiveness. If the victim is not mature, the relationship will experience another sin: the offended person will become an offender.

This is a common scenario in relationships. For Mable to work through her anger, she will need to start the process of repentance and work her way down to the point of asking Biff to forgive her of her anger. Everything that has been written thus far is about the neutralization and removal of sin. These are prerequisite steps that must happen before two people can genuinely reconcile.

If they do not successfully navigate through these six steps, their sin remains, and reconciliation will never happen.

It is common for a couple to come to counseling with step eight (reconciliation) in mind, while they have not done steps one through six. It's the equivalent to building a house on a nuclear waste dump. There is no hope for them if they are unwilling to neutralize and remove the waste in their marriage.

If you try to help two people get along with each other but they have not humbly, authentically, and successfully gone through the preceding steps, do not be surprised if your effort does not work.

Step Seven – Post-forgiveness

You cannot mask sin or pretend it does not exist. You will know if they can move forward after forgiveness by how they react to each other, specifically as they talk about what happened.

Biblical forgiveness removes sin just like when God forgave you by removing your sin and dropping it in the depths of the sea, never to be held against you again. If Biff and Mable have removed the sin between them, they can come together with nothing hindering authentic reconciliation. The key to this step is your willingness to talk about what happened.

Step Eight – Reconciliation

They are ready to come together because there is nothing between them. It's a true family hug. They are reconciled, which is not the same as restoration. Reconciliation brings two people together while restoration is the process of addressing what went wrong with the hope of implementing a plan to keep from becoming a repeat offender.

The Restoration Process

Step Nine – Restoration

At this point, Biff and Mable can work together to restore their relationship with God and each other. The thing that brought division between them has been neutralized. The power of the gospel has been powerful for them.

Steps nine through twelve is where the process of repentance kicks into full gear. In most cases, the sin committed was committed numerous times. Repeat offenses are what makes this next section so helpful. They need to be fully restored (Galatians 6:1–2). Too often, people go through the "I'm sorry" thing, which disables them from helping each other stop the ongoing patterns of sin in their lives.

Saying "I'm sorry" can move the relationship along, but it will not change the relationship or change you. "I'm sorry" is a passive statement that does not require active repentance. "Will you forgive me" is sin actively owned, confessed, and followed up with specific steps to change.

Step Ten – Put Off

With the sin nailed to Christ's cross, you can now talk about it, which is the litmus test that will tell you if it has been adequately confessed and forgiven. If you cannot talk about what you did, the sin still has a life. But if you have put it to death on Christ's cross, you can begin talking about and learning from what you did wrong.

You want to kill the sin so you can put it off fully. You don't want to keep doing the same thing over and over again. Your objective is to kill it and practice putting it off. It is best to do this in a community. If you are married, your spouse is the best person to help you stop doing sinful things.

Step Eleven – Renew Your Mind

All sin starts in the heart (Luke 6:45; James 1:14–15). While it is wise to amputate sinful behaviors (Matthew 5:29–30), it is transformative to cut the sin out at its root (Romans 8:13). Your thoughts must be captivated by the power of the gospel (2 Corinthians 10:3–6; Philippians 4:8). Without a change in your soul, your actions will never change long-term.

Step Twelve – Put On

If your sin is dead and the other person is not trying to resurrect it, you can work together on removing the underlying causes that give vitality to the sin. If you are not willing to work together by removing the future possibility of sin's attempt to disrupt your lives, it will most definitely reappear, and the cycle of frustration will continue while cutting deeper ruts into your souls.

One of the amazing things about the power of the gospel is how you can sin against someone and the person you sinned against comes alongside you to help you overcome the sin. Like Jesus, former enemies are now co-laborers in the fight against sin.

Step Thirteen – Disciple Others

Removing sin, reconciling with God and others, and living a holy life is not full repentance. The first twelve steps prepare you to make your repentance complete. God has called you to do more than getting right with Him and others. He wants you to help others get right, too. This is at the heart of the Great Commission (Matthew 28:19–20)

If you make it this far in the sin-removing process, do not stop. Go and serve others. Make disciples. Share what you have learned and applied with the hope others will follow you (1 Corinthians 11:1; Ephesians 5:1). Full repentance moves you from being self-centered to being others-centered.

"Let the thief no longer steal, but rather let him labor, doing honest work with his own hands, so that he may have something to share with anyone in need" (Ephesians 4:28).

Call to Action

1. What does repentance look like in your life and relationships?

2. As you think through these thirteen steps, is there a step you do not practice?

3. Steps 1–6 are the killing of your sin. How effective are you in actively working out those steps?

4. Steps 7–13 are the removal of your sin. Are you learning how to stop being a repeat offender?

5. Who is in your life to help you work out your salvation in practical and transformative ways?

Chapter 17

Five Marks of Change

What is the truest indicator of a person who has authentically changed? How can you know—as much as one can know? Paul gives us our answers, but first, let me tell you a story.

Sin had captured Phil.

He repented of his sin. His wife was unsure if Phil truly had changed. The reason she was unsure was that Phil did not appear to be different. He was not doing what he was doing before, but that was about it. She had a nagging anxiousness that he would go back to his old ways. It was not the first time he had "repented" of sin, which is why her hope was minimal as she fearfully guarded her heart.

Understandably, she did not want to be hurt again, but it was also evident she was struggling to put more faith in God than in her husband's ability to stay changed. She wondered, "If I could have assurances he will not do it again . . . Is that too much to ask? Has he repented this time?"

It's not too much to ask, but let me ask you this: What is the truest indicator of a person who has authentically changed? How can you know—as much as one can know—if a person has changed? Paul gives us our answers in Ephesians. Let's break it down.

"To put off your old self, which belongs to your former manner of life and is corrupt through deceitful desires, and to be renewed in the spirit of your minds, and to put on the new self, created after the likeness of God in true righteousness and holiness" (Ephesians 4:22–24).

Out With the Old – In With the New

Paul told the Christians in Ephesus that they had a former manner of life. Though there are several things to consider from Paul's teaching in this text, I want to draw out two of them.

1. They were Christians.
2. Those Christian people had a former manner of life.

Did you catch that? He was talking to born again, saved, regenerated, blood-bought, washed Christians who still struggled with temptations toward wicked, evil, sinful, and futile lives (Ephesians 4:17–22).

They were saints tempted to shrink back and sin. Paul called those believers to put off their former manner of life—that lifestyle of unrighteousness they were tempted to yield to in moments of weakness. He was calling them to walk no longer as the pagan Gentiles walked (Ephesians 4:17).

Paul perceived the saint/sinner tension. He understood that Christians do sin (1 John 1:7–9), and he wanted to encourage them toward change (Romans 2:4). Guess what? You and I are not entirely sanctified either, which is why Paul's teaching on how to change as a post-salvation Christian is so helpful. So may I ask you:

1. Are you daily putting off the old person?
2. Are you actively renewing your inner person?
3. Are you practically putting on a new lifestyle that is antithetically different from your former manner of life?

I am not going to unpack those three verses, but I do want to go where Paul took them—the application phase of those verses, which is the rest of the chapter. Paul informs us in the remaining verses what to look for in a person who has genuinely changed. Here is his sequential logic:

1. Put off your former manner of life (v. 22).

2. Renew your inner person, the genesis of your sinfulness (v. 23).

3. Put on a new life that is like God—true right living and true holiness (v. 24).

4. You will know if real, right living and holiness are working in you by the practical life you live before God and others (vv. 25–32).

You Know You Have Changed When

Paul did not want to leave you with vague applications of true right living and true holiness, which is what would have happened if he stopped at Ephesians 4:24. You need more than conceptual language; you need practical language.

Without application, you would have to speculate on the kind of repentance he was asking you to model. Fortunately, you will not have to speculate. He gives you four practical illustrations of what it means to authentically and effectually put off, renew, and put on a new lifestyle.

1. The lying person stops his lying and begins to bless others with the truth (v. 25).

2. The thief stops taking from individuals and becomes a proactive giver (v. 28).

3. The corrupting talker stops crude speech and begins to build up others with his tongue (v. 29).

4. The harsh, bitter person puts away bitterness while spreading kindness to others (v. 31).

Change is not complete repentance if you only stop doing bad things. You will know if repentance happened to someone by the proactive, practical, gospel-motivated blessings they provide to other people. Jesus did not come to earth just to help you stop sinning. He had a higher vision.

He wants you to go beyond the putting off phase of your sanctification, which you can authenticate by your dying to yourself and living for others. Repentance is more than conceptual; it is practical. Actual repentance moves a person from selfishness to selflessness. True change is long-term and a sustained others-centered living for the glory of God.

Motivated By the Gospel

Note Paul's carefulness. He knew religious people could do good works. He used to be one of those religious people (Philippians 3:3–6). Thus, he pressed the issue further. You see this at the end of his practical application speech in verse 32, as he wrapped up his entire argument for change by tying repentance directly to the gospel.

It is essential for you to see this. Any person can do good works, but only a person riveted to and motivated by the gospel can consistently glorify God by their works.

"Be kind to one another, tender-hearted, forgiving one another, as God in Christ forgave you" (Ephesians 4:32).

Paul connected all of your work requirements (obedience) to a gospel motive by saying, "As God in Christ forgave you." All work—regardless of what it may be—is motivated by something. Paul wanted to make sure he did not create a bunch of nice behaving Christians, whose motives found motivation from something other than the gospel.

True change will find its motive rooted in the gospel of Jesus Christ, and it will manifest as a penitent person actively living out the following five marks of attitudes and behaviors:

1. Mark One: You are actively putting off your former manner of life (v. 22).
2. Mark Two: You are actively renewing the spirit of your mind (v. 23).

3. Mark Three: You are actively pursuing true righteousness and true holiness (v. 24).

4. Mark Four: You are actively and practically living out righteousness and holiness (vv. 25–32).

5. Mark Five: Your behavior is motivated and sustained by the gospel (v. 32).

Sustained By the Gospel

Paul's template for change has an aggressive quality to it, which is the opposite of the more common, lukewarm Christian experience. Any Christianized person can somewhat do steps one through four and even appear to be changed based on observable behavior. A lack of gospel authenticity is why it is essential for you not to miss Paul's gospel connection. He connected all of life to the gospel.

If a person's heart motive is not rooted in the gospel, his behaviors—no matter how good they may appear—will not last. True righteousness and true holiness flow from and find sustainability in the gospel—the person and work of Jesus Christ.

I am not suggesting for you to be a cynic or even suspicious of anyone who says they repented. The potential of change is not a call to be judgmental but a call to be discerning. It would be wrong to say, "Just wait. We'll see if it's real or not." It would also be a mistake not to have humble and wise biblical expectations. Love believes all things and hopes all things, but love is not naive regarding Adamic tendencies (1 Corinthians 13:4–7).

Six Reasons For No Repentance

There could be situations in Phil's life where it appears he repented, but he retreats to his old former manner of life. Perchance that is true, it is imperative for his wife to grasp fully what may be going on with him, as well as her understanding of what God may be doing in his life.

151

Typically, a lack of repentance has more than one possibility. Did you know that God can multitask? Think of Moses and Pharaoh here: Pharaoh's lack of repentance was part of God's plan (Exodus 9:16; Romans 9:17). A person's unwillingness to change is not outside of God's redemptive purposes. Maybe like Pharaoh, there is a greater purpose in a lack of true repentance. Here are six considerations for you:

1 – He may not know how to repent – Do not be surprised by this. My children do not know how to repent fully. I did not know how to repent until I became an adult. How many active, sin-engaging repenters do you know? Compare that number with how many Christians you know. I suspect there is a difference. A big difference.

Not knowing how to change was the story of the Ethiopian eunuch. He had his Bible opened and in his lap but struggled to understand it. He needed help. He needed to collaborate with someone (Acts 8:30–31).

Some people talk about the Bible like it is a magic book. It is a powerful book, but it is not a magic book. In the wisdom of God, He chose the agency of humankind to cooperate with His Word and Spirit to help people change.

2 – An alluring sin may have caught him – While I am not dismissing personal responsibility for change, I am also not dismissing the call for corporate responsibility. It takes a church. You are to be part of the process. There are many Christians caught in sin who do not know how to escape (Galatians 6:1).

Caught people have a hard time repenting (James 1:14–15). Sin is alluring, and if a person has given most of his life over to satisfying his selfish desires, there is a possibility he will return to his sin. He needs your help.

3 – The Lord is maturing you – Paul tells you to guard your heart when helping people caught in sin (Galatians 6:1–2). If you do not protect your heart, you will be culpable as you pile on top of his sin.

It is easy to sin against those you care for, especially when they are not changing according to your timetable, expectations, desires, or agendas. The wise and humble person will be asking, "What can I learn from this? What does the Lord want to teach me in this relationship?"

4 – The Lord is submitting you to your calling – Perchance your friend does not change, it is imperative for you to remember your calling (1 Peter 2:21).

The Lord's calling leads to death (Matthew 16:24). It could be the person with whom you struggle the most is God's kindness to you, as He uses that person to reorient your heart back to Him.

5 – What you need will control you – The thing you believe you need will control you, and you will know what controls you by how you respond to life's situations or the difficult people in your life.

When I sin against my wife, at that moment I believe I need whatever it is I am frustrated about, e.g., desires for love, appreciation, respect, and approval. If those things are where my heart is focused, not getting those things will cause me to respond sinfully to her.

If I reorient my heart toward God and if I am being satisfied in Him alone, her behavior—good or bad—will have no ongoing control over me. If anyone other than God is controlling me, idolatry will capture me. My wife—at least for now—is being used by God to reveal my idolatry.

God can use sin sinlessly, and if you are sinning due to unmet expectations from another person, be sure to know that Sovereign God is working for you by calling you to repentance.

6 – You must know God is good – Regardless of how things shake out, you must be unflinching in your awareness that God is good and He is working good in your life—even if you cannot perceive it.

Moses could not have put up with the shenanigans of Pharaoh if he was not in faith for the process, believing God was working out something good for him and others. His faith was rooted in God alone, and yours must be, too.

Repentance is a tricky thing, and the truth is that we cannot ultimately tell if anyone has authentically changed. Repentance is God's responsibility to grant (2 Timothy 2:25). Our responsibility is to rest in His sovereign care over our lives. If your affection is in God alone, you will be okay regardless of what others do.

Call to Action

1. Do you know how to repent fully? Can you break down the process?
2. Are you part of a church that is humbly transparent about their sin struggles?
3. Are you a humble and compassionate friend to your struggling friends?
4. How are you maturing in Christ through the struggles of your friends?
5. Based on your responses to your difficult relationships, what would you say controls you?

Chapter 18

Pre-Forgiveness Comes First

Take my little test on genuine forgiveness: After you forgave the person, were you able to talk about the hurt in such a way that communicated you were no longer sinfully controlled by those hurts—whether you were talking with God, yourself, or the offender?

A sign of complete biblical forgiveness is when you can be hurt, grant forgiveness, and talk about what happened to you without being sinfully controlled by the actions of those who hurt you. Though granting forgiveness can be a better version of how our culture works through their relational problems, it can be no more effective if the forgiveness is not authentic.

A struggle to be authentic with the offender does not mean your forgiveness granting was not genuine, but it could mean your forgiveness is not complete if you cannot genuinely let it go.

True Forgiveness Illustrated

"As for you, you meant evil against me, but God meant it for good, to bring it about that many people should be kept alive, as they are today" (Genesis 50:20).

The speaker in this verse is Joseph, the son of Jacob. He is talking to his brothers who initially tried to kill him but changed their collective minds and sold him to a ragtag group of slave traders.

Joseph spent thirteen mostly horrible years away from his family while being accused of a crime he did not commit, which landed him in jail. During jail time, he was betrayed by those who could help him. It's hard to fully understand what all happened to Joseph. Any one of those incidents during his thirteen years would be enough to ruin his thoughts about God and life, for the rest of his life.

When you break into the story at Genesis 50:20, he finally has a chance to let his brothers know what he thought about their victimization of him. After thirteen astonishing years, Joseph has his first opportunity to face the original instigators of his hardships.

His response was forgiveness. Amazing grace. Joseph was ready for the moment. His heart was prepared by the Lord to grant the long overdue forgiveness to his persecutors.

What Is Pre-forgiveness?

What we don't see in this story is the prerequisite heart work necessary for Joseph to be willing, gracious, and genuine to forgive his offenders. There is no question he had to do business with God before he could do business with his brothers.

Missing this essential step in the forgiveness process is to miss the opportunity of going the distance with someone who needs your forgiveness. What makes this step so important is that it gives you time to perceive the Lord's thoughts—as much as His thoughts can be ascertained—about what happened to you (Isaiah 55:8–9).

You must reasonably establish a theologically precise understanding of God in your mind while convinced He is working good (Romans 8:28) in your life—even if it is in ways you did not expect or have not perceived up to this point in your narrative. This process to genuine forgiveness is the prerequisite work of pre-forgiveness.

When bad things happen to me, the only way I can process and accept them correctly is after I have gained sovereign clarity on my troubles. Joseph had sovereign clarity.

1. Do you have sovereign clarity on the disappointments in your life?

2. When you review the movie of your life, can you see with sovereign clarity?

If you cannot trust God's good work on your behalf, you will be a candidate for harboring such things as bitterness, anger, anxiety, discouragement, criticism, resentment, cynicism, and even hate toward those who have hurt you.

Not being anchored by God's sovereign care of your life will make you like a kite in the wind. It is imperative that the Lord is your anchor point as sin angles to capture you. Here are a few of the ways sin tries to ensnare its prey after someone does a dastardly deed to you.

1. Your emotions enslave you as you continue to dwell on the actions of the offending person.
2. Your thoughts fixate on the hurt and what the person did to you.
3. You struggle to process the nature of the relationship you have with the person.
4. Your attitude toward the offender ensnares you.
5. There is a relational awkwardness between you and the offender.
6. Your heart swirls in fluctuating desires as you try to gain clarity from the Lord.

Pre-forgiveness Illustrated

Leone's husband committed adultery. It was the most devastating news of her life. It took many months of biblical care, among many friends, in the context of her local church to help her walk through the crushing anguish of her heart. She called it her nightmare from hell.

When Cal repented, he eventually came back to Leone to ask for her forgiveness. (His forgiveness was genuine; God changed Cal's heart.) What he did not know was that Leone had already "done business with God." She was ready to grant forgiveness. Her brand of forgiveness was more than her

Christian duty. It was a God-centered, grace-empowered, gospel-motivated forgiveness.

Leone was like Joseph. When the time came for forgiveness, the hard work of pre-forgiveness was over, and she was willing to grant genuine forgiveness. It was the incredible power of the gospel that was working in her heart.

The Back Story–What You Did Not Know

Leone had been praying for nearly fifteen years that God would make their marriage complete. They had sex while dating, and though she never felt right about marrying Cal, it seemed like a better option than staying single. She was lonely. After their marriage, she became lonelier.

Because of Cal's ongoing bouts with anger, their three sons were living in rebellion toward God. Cal and Leone were also struggling financially. They professed to be Christians though their church commitment was nominal. In God's autonomous and non-manipulatable timeframe, He answered Leone's fifteen-year prayer request to fix her marriage. What did He do? He blew it up. God dropped a bomb in the middle of their marriage and blew it to smithereens.

It's impossible to adequately describe the devastation on Leone and the children, especially if you have not lived it. From all perspectives, it made no sense. To find good or God in their mess was an incredible leap in human logic (1 Corinthians 1:25). As the numbness began to wear off, Leone began to seek God's thoughts on what was happening in her life, marriage, and family. That was when she came to the story of Joseph.

In Whose Story Are You Living?

Leone learned that God not only worked in the present, but He planned for the future. What Joseph and his family could not know was that there was going to be a famine in the land and the sovereign Lord needed someone in Egypt to set up things so that He could preserve the nation of Israel.

As you know, God was not just doing this for the nation of Israel or Joseph's family. He was doing this because of His promise to Adam (Genesis 3:15) and to Abraham (Genesis 12:1–3). Humanity needed a Savior (Galatians 4:4), and that Savior was going to come through Jacob's lineage.

The bomb the good Lord dropped in Jacob's family flung Joseph to Egypt. According to God's predetermined plan, He scripted bad things into Joseph's life. Tossed in the crucible of suffering is what Joseph and Leone believed the Lord was up to with them, which motivated them to give up trying to control their respective stories while humbly stepping into God's story. Joseph and Leone had sovereign clarity. It did not mitigate the pain or the dysfunction, but it did give them hope.

After they had come to that place in their understanding, they were ready to move forward with God's new plans for their lives. The situation became less about what was happening to them and more about what God was doing through them.

1. When you think through your disappointments, are you more aware of and affected by what God is doing, or are you more aware of and impacted by who did what to you?

2. Can you humbly let go of the narrative you have been holding to and grasp the script that God is writing for you?

There were three things that Joseph shared with his brothers:

1. What God did was for good.
2. What they did was for evil.
3. God's good trumped their evil.

Therefore, he was able to forgive his brothers for what they did to him.

1. What controls your heart: What God allowed or what the offender did?

2. Where do you put the accent mark: On the good of God or on the evil of a person?

How you answer those questions will determine the depth and quality of your forgiveness. If you cannot get to where Joseph was, you will not be able to release those who have sinned against you. One of the ways you can check your heart regarding your forgiveness of others for what they did to you is how you think about what they did to you and how you talk about them.

Right thinking about personal suffering is where the gospel must have a greater grip on you than what others have done to you. One of the ways you can practicalize the gospel is how you perceive the offenses of others in light of your offenses against the Lord.

The cross of Christ has a way of downsizing the offenses of others by giving me a proper perspective on my actions against God. If the same gospel that saved my soul cannot overcome the disappointment from others, the "gospelization" of my heart is not yet complete.

Forgiveness flows out of a softened heart. The longer you stand before the Holy Lord you offended, the better it will go for you when you stand before the one who offended you. If you have done this well, you are in a good place to forgive the person who hurt you. The power of the gospel makes forgiveness real and practical.

Restoring Relationships

Pre-forgiveness will not come easy. Getting your thoughts straightened out and aligned with God's ways is the hardest part. Forgiveness is typically not the most challenging aspect if you have wrestled through pre-forgiveness.

Note how Joseph was ready to forgive his brothers. He had thirteen years to figure this out with the Lord. I am not suggesting you need thirteen years to figure it out, but you must understand this concept—no matter how long it takes.

If you do the hard work of pre-forgiveness, when the time comes for forgiveness, it will not be as difficult. However, if it is hard, you need to spend more time before the Lord because some residual anger toward Him and others is more than likely operating in your heart.

We are all sovereigntists. Whether we consciously think about it or not, we all know there is a God and He is ultimately in control of all things. Therefore, if you cannot forgive others for what happened to you, there is an underlying issue that needs to be resolved between you and God first.

Once you have sovereign clarity and you can freely forgive the person who hurt you, then you will be able to go beyond the hurt by genuinely reconciling with the offender. Freedom to forgive is the good part, but it gets better.

When Lucia and I "make up" in the way I have described here, we begin talking about the sin that separated us. The sin that made us slaves is now serving us. The sin becomes a practical working illustration we can talk about to grow and mature to the point where we reduce the amount of future sinning against each other.

It should not be difficult to talk about sin if it has been neutralized by the power of the gospel. Killing it dead is vital because it is important to revisit our past sins in nonpunitive ways so that we can learn from our mistakes.

Call to Action

Note the Process:

1. Pre-forgiveness – allowing God to adjust your heart so you can forgive.
2. Forgiveness – genuinely granting forgiveness to someone who hurt you.
3. Reconciling – Sin no longer separates you from the other person.

4. Maturing – You neutralize the sin so you can discuss it with the hope that you don't do it again.

Just as Joseph could talk to his brothers in a nonpunitive way about what they did to him, you should be able to have similar discussions with your friends who sin against you. God answered Leone's prayer by blowing up her marriage, and she had enough sovereign clarity to accept and respond to her marital disappointment. That was seven years ago.

Those dark days have been swallowed up by the incredibly selfless and God-glorifying marriage she and Cal have today. Though she was the one who was offended, she had a significant role to play in the restoration of her marriage. It began with the preparatory work in her heart. She was ready to forgive.

1. Has someone sinned against you?
2. Are you able to forgive, if they were to ask for your forgiveness?
3. If you are ready to humbly forgive, whether they ever ask you to forgive them, you are free from their sin.

(This chapter is about transactional forgiveness that you give to an offender who genuinely repents. There are times when all you can do is forgive attitudinally because the offender has not authentically repented.)

Chapter 19

Hardest Way to Help Someone

Someone upsets you. The friend objectively and legitimately does something wrong. It is real. It's an unbiblical action. They hurt you. Their behavior is an offense to you and the Lord. To compound the problem, it's not the first time they hurt you. An episode you may overlook, but this is a pattern. Your friend's manner of interacting with you frustrates you continually, and you are at a loss as to how to fix them.

What do you do? You get mad.

But you're not just mad. You hope the person will change. You care for them. Your desires to not be hurt and to help are mixed. Motivating a person to change is not an easy process. Part of the problem is that you're not able to change them. No matter how hard you pray, talk, or fuss, there is one constant: You cannot change people.

- A husband cannot change a wife.
- A woman cannot change her husband.
- A parent cannot change a child.
- A child cannot change a parent.

Four Clarifying Passages

Passage One:

"I planted, Apollos watered, but God gave the growth" (1 Corinthians 3:6).

The most effective and loving thing you can do for another person is careful planting and watering of God's Word in his or her life. You don't want to go beyond that. You can't go beyond that. If you try to make them grow (change), your efforts will blow-up in your face.

1. What does it mean for you to be God's water boy (or girl)?
2. Are you at peace helping someone change while working within the parameters of watering and planting?

Passage Two:

"And the Lord's servant must not be quarrelsome but kind to everyone, able to teach, patiently enduring evil, correcting his opponents with gentleness. God may perhaps grant them repentance leading to a knowledge of the truth" (2 Timothy 2:24–25).

Repentance is a gift from the Lord, not from a counselor, pastor, spouse, parent, or friend. If anyone other than God could bring change in a person's life, it would circumvent the glory that belongs exclusively to Him.

1. Is your soul at rest as you patiently wait on the Lord to change someone?
2. Are your thoughts captivated by Christ as you think about the possibility of someone never changing?

Passage Three:

"Why do you see the speck that is in your brother's eye, but do not notice the log that is in your own eye? Or how can you say to your brother, 'Let me take the speck out of your eye,' when there is the log in your own eye? You hypocrite, first take the log out of your own eye, and then you will see clearly to take the speck out of your brother's eye" (Matthew 7:3–5).

Because you cannot change anyone, the most effective place to begin thinking about your relationship with another person is with you. The key idea from Matthew is how the log is always in your eye, not in the other person's eye. If your starting point for change is not with you, the result will spin you and the other person into ongoing relational dysfunction. If you try to change them before you carefully address your heart, both of you will stew in anger.

1. What does it mean to address the log in your eye before you examine the speck in another person's eye?

2. What hinders you from self-assessment before assessing someone else?

Passage Four:

"What causes quarrels and what causes fights among you? Is it not this, that your passions are at war within you? You desire and do not have, so you murder. You covet and cannot obtain, so you fight and quarrel" *(James 4:1–2a).*

James gave us three synonyms for why a person becomes sinfully angry with another person: passions, desires, and covetousness. You find these three ideas in the angry person's heart. Knowing where to look for anger is a valuable insight when building relationally. If you are sinfully mad at another person, you want to address the source of your anger.

James says the source is in your heart, not with the other person. He further clarifies the origin as desires, passions, and covetousness, meaning that you're not getting what you want so you're mad about it.

Going the Wrong Direction

Whenever you sin in response to what you are not getting, even if that thing you want is good, you are wrong and need to repent before you engage the other person about what is wrong in your relationship.

This idea is a watershed principle that must be biblically engaged before you do anything else. Think of being upset as being at the apex of a hill and what you do next will send you in one of two directions.

If you persist in addressing the other person's problem first, you will not only tell the other person what to change, but you will become the main, active change agent in his or her life. You will become the person's functional god. You can see this if you compare what you are trying to do with what only the Lord can do. (See table.)

I say you have a problem	God says you have a problem
I say you need to change	God says you need to change
I say what needs to change	God says what needs to change
I will change you	God may change you
I will force you to change	God may help you change

Some will argue how they have the right perspective about what is wrong with the other person, and all that person needs to do is change. They may be correct, at least partially. The main issue in view here is not what they can somewhat see but what they cannot see. There are at least five things they cannot see:

1. They have the wrong attitude toward the person. – I am sinfully upset with you (James 4:1–3).
2. They have not carefully addressed or changed their hearts first (Matthew 7:3–5).
3. They cannot see the person's heart to exactly know what areas need changing (Hebrews 4:12–13).
4. They have not tried to help the person in a spirit of gentleness (Galatians 6:1–2).

5. Regardless of their perspective, they cannot change the other person (2 Timothy 2:24–25).

Going the Right Direction

Biff is upset with Mable. She has done a dumb thing, and Biff is correct in his observations about what she did. Mable should change to restore her fellowship with the Lord and Biff. That point is not arguable. But there are some problems in Biff's perspective about how he should cooperate with the Lord in Mable's change process.

The most prominent thing is that he is more aware of her failures than his own. He is so caught up in his rightness that he cannot see his wrongness. His rightness blinds him to his wrongness. His wrongness is unwittingly dismantling whatever truth is in his arguments. He's shooting himself in the foot. Before he can join the Lord's restorative efforts in Mable's life, he will

I am upset with you

I have a problem	You have a problem
I need to change	You need to change
What do I need to change	What do you need to change
I cannot change	You will change
God help me	I will make you

The LORD gives grace to the humble, but opposes the proud. (cf. James 4:6)

167

have to adjust his heart. The implication from Paul's teaching is that this is the law of Christ (Galatians 6:1–2).

Biff is angry—a self-righteous posture before the Lord and his wife. Biff is blind. He does not understand how to help his wife change. He thinks Mable can change according to his preferences and timetable, which is why he is forcing her to change. Paul said a person like Biff is quarrelsome (2 Timothy 2:24–25).

Mable cannot change the way Biff thinks she should or when Biff thinks she should, and the more he tries to foist his preferences on her, the more he is going to compound and complicate their marriage. There is a better way for marital problem-solving. Here is a short snippet of what Biff needs to do to cooperate with the Lord in the restoration of his wife:

1. Mable has a problem.
2. Biff needs to help her.
3. Biff cannot help her until he successfully addresses his heart.
4. Biff needs to change first.
5. Biff needs to identify what he needs to change:
   - Biff is angry, which means there are passions, desires, and coveting in his heart.
   - Biff is blind to his sin as he is pressing his wife to change.
   - Biff is self-righteous—a greater than/better than attitude toward Mable.
   - Biff is in opposition to God because Christ did not come for righteous people (James 4:6; Luke 5:32).
   - Biff is worse off than he ever imagined.
   - Biff needs the transformative power of Jesus working in his heart.
   - Biff needs a divine undoing.

When Isaiah saw the LORD high and lifted up, he became undone (Isaiah 6:1–6).

"Woe is me! For I am [undone]; for I am a man of unclean lips, and I dwell in the midst of a people of unclean lips; for my eyes have seen the King, the Lord of hosts!" (Isaiah 6:5).

Let me paraphrase this passage by using Biff and Mable's marriage as the template:

Woe is me! For I, Biff, am undone; for I am a man of unclean lips, and I dwell in a marriage with a person of unclean lips; for my eyes have seen the King, the LORD of hosts! (Isaiah 6:5 RTV)

Biff must come to "Isaiah's place" in his relationship with Mable, to where he is broken completely regarding his sin. Then he will be able to become a means of grace to her. The irony is that Biff is trying to force Mable to do what he cannot do himself: he is as challenged to change himself as Mable is to change herself. Biff is a pious, self-deceived, self-reliant man trying to impose change on his wife while he is not able to change himself.

First Things First

Biff must address his heart by identifying why he is so upset. From there, he can begin the process of change on himself. As he does this, he will realize how hard it is to change. Starting with myself has historically been one of the most difficult lessons for me to learn.

1. I want someone to change.
2. I sin in the process.
3. I begin addressing my sinful heart.
4. I realize how hard it is for me to change.

5. I begin to show pity for the person that I want to see change.

6. We both stand in need of God's transforming gospel.

If the Lord grants Biff the gift of repentance, he will be in the best possible place to serve his wife. God appreciates and empowers the broken, humble heart.

"The sacrifices of God are a broken spirit; a broken and contrite heart, O God, you will not despise" (Psalm 51:17).

There is a chance Mable may never change, but if Biff's brokenness is genuine, whatever is wrong with her will not have so much control over him. At least her problems will not tempt him to sin (James 1:14–15). Biff will be free while in the bondage of a broken relationship. Like Paul or Joseph in their prisons, Biff will be able to rejoice (Acts 16:25).

Call to Action

1. Have you tried to change someone?

2. God is the only person who can change anyone. Are you resting and hoping in the Lord's work in those you'd like to see change?

3. Do your good desires tempt you to press too hard for change in someone's life?

4. Have you fallen into the rightness trap, to the point it has blinded you to your wrongness?

5. What would hinder you from changing first? What do you need to do?

Chapter 20

Powerful Way to Help Someone

Your friend needs to change. How do you help her change? Maybe your husband is stuck in a bad habit, and you want him to change. What is your change process? Perhaps your wife is nagging and criticizing you. How are you helping her model a more gentle and caring spirit?

There are several ways to motivate a person to change. Here are a few approaches that come to mind. As you go through this list, examine your heart to see which ones you tend to employ when someone is not changing according to your expectations.

1. The Shame Approach – pointing out how dumb that thing was he did
2. The Guilt Approach – comparing the person's poor behavior with someone else's good behavior
3. The Threat Approach – yelling the consequences of the person's sin if he continues in it
4. The Condemnation Approach – putting him down or making fun of him in front of others
5. The Critical Approach – always pointing out his faults, no matter how small they may be
6. The Cynical Approach – Though he may have done something good, you know his intent was selfish.

How did you do? Did you see yourself in any of those approaches? I think it would be good to ask your spouse, your children, or a few close friends how they characterize you when it comes to how you motivate a person to change. Will you ask others for their observations about you?

All of the approaches I have suggested can work. They can be effective in any context where there is an authority/subordinate construct. If you use them on children, they can be quite useful. The problem is when the children become taller, bigger, older, smarter, and more independent.

At that point, your manipulations will not be as useful. If you are not careful, these methods will motivate your children to become angry teenagers. You may even push them out of your life. This parenting model is what has been called exasperating a child. You can also irritate your spouse and friends.

Are you an exasperating person? If any of these methods are the ones you employ, you may be an exasperating person. If you continue to use these methods, your relationships will be weak, strained, and non-redemptive.

Let's say your observations are correct about what you see in the person you want to see changed. Let's say your husband, wife, child, or friend does need to change. Having the right observations does not automatically mean your methods for change are correct. There is a process for change found in the Bible, and it can be redemptively effective. This approach finds its anchor in the gospel.

Got Niceness?

There are many ways to say it, but for now, I am going to simplify by calling it being nice. How are you doing at being nice to the people who are not meeting your expectations? (cf. Matthew 5:44–45; Luke 6:27) Some will object by saying, "I've tried this method, and it did not work."

May I ask, is your being nice primarily about results that benefit you, or is it primarily about imitating your heavenly Father by being redemptive in the lives of others? The person who says, "I've tried it, and it did not work" is leaning toward conditionalism: "I will love you if you meet my expectations."

They are looking for a method or an approach to get what they want. Individuals like this have a strong results orientation rather than a gospel orientation. The truth is there are only two options:

1. Be nice to others.
2. Don't be nice to others. (cf. Matthew 22:36–40; Philippians 2:3–4).

What will it be? Who will you be? The point about being nice should primarily be about your desire to magnify God's name by putting His Son on display in the context of your relationships. You want to make His name fantastically great for His glory and the benefit of others.

If perchance, you get good results because you were nice to others, praise God for the good results. Personal blessings that come to you for loving God and others more than yourself is a thing to be praised, not an idol to be worshiped.

Do You Have Gospel Amnesia?

A person who chooses not to be nice is a person who does not have an accurate and practical understanding of the gospel. For the Christian, this is gospel amnesia.

"Then his master summoned him and said to him, 'You wicked servant! I forgave you all that debt because you pleaded with me. And should not you have had mercy on your fellow-servant, as I had mercy on you?'" (Matthew 18:32–33).

The context of this story is about a man who owed 10,000 talents, and he pleaded with his master to forgive him of the debt he owed. The master showed mercy and forgave him all his debt. This forgiven servant shortly thereafter began to assail a man who owed him far less—one hundred denarii.

When the master found out how mean this guy was to someone who owed far less than what he was forgiven, the master was angry with the servant. The unforgiving servant lapsed into gospel amnesia. The master said, "Should not you have had mercy on your fellow-servant, as I had mercy on you?"

Here is my question to you: shouldn't you have mercy on others because of the kindness showed to you? Let's go at it this way. Let's take a short gospel test. How you answer these questions will reveal your understanding and application of the gospel:

1. Who is the biggest sinner you know? If you say anyone other than yourself, you may have gospel amnesia. (cf. Matthew 7:3–5; 1 Timothy 1:15)

2. Do you believe what someone did to you is worse than what you did to the Savior?

3. Is there someone in your life with which you are angry, frustrated, or impatient?

How you answered those questions reveals your functional understanding and application of the gospel. If you are more stuck on what someone has done to you rather than what you have done to Christ, you are a problem-centered, self-centered Christian, rather than a gospel-centered one.

If you believe another person is a worse sinner than you are, you will not be able to help that person change effectively. You will be tempted to employ some of the approaches mentioned earlier. Those methods will be your understanding and practice of a theology of change. My friend, none of them will work.

How did you change? There is a biblical method for change that your Father would want you to use to help others transform. I call this the encouragement approach. Think about this for a moment. What motivated you to change?

Though you probably did not think about it this way, the reason and motivation for your change were because of God's kindness. That is why I changed, too. God was kind to me. My Father regenerated me in 1984. Though I did not know John 3:16, or any other verse in the Bible at that time, I realized He was offering kindness to me. Though I did not put it in those words, mercy is what I perceived from the Lord.

God was offering His Son as a replacement and payment for every sin I ever committed or will ever commit. I accepted His offering to me, and the change process began. Even though we are many years since that day, He is still employing the encouragement approach.

His methodology of change has never changed (Hebrews 13:8). It was the kindness of God that changed me then, and it is the kindness of God that changes me now. Listen to Paul.

"Do you presume on the riches of his kindness, forbearance, and patience, not knowing that God's kindness is meant to lead you to repentance" (Romans 2:4)?

The answer to Paul's question is assumed. He is saying, "You know this, right?" His assumption is that you do know this. Let me ask you: Do you know this? Are you aware it was God's kindness that led to your change (repentance)?

Paul is also warning us not to take God's kindness for granted. Are you presuming on His kindness? Have you taken it for granted? Have you forgotten how He changed you and how He is changing you?

God's Riches Given to Others

Give thought to the conjunction "and" in Paul's verse. He is talking about the riches of His kindness, the riches of His forbearance, and the riches of His patience. These are the things the Father employs to transform us. Are you employing the riches of God's kindness, forbearance, and patience to help your friends change?

If you are not employing these riches but are choosing to implement the ungodly approaches mentioned at the beginning, you are whistling in the wind. The change will not come to your friends, and your relationship with them will continue to sputter.

Rather than nickel and diming a person to death or constantly reminding them of their faults or where they got it wrong, it seems like the encouragement approach is a better idea. Don't you think it is a better idea?

"What about sin? What do I do when they sin?"

The encouragement approach does not mean you should overlook sin. We should not ignore when a person sins, not at all. But finding fault is not hard for most of us. It is easy to see when someone sins. I think I have a gift for observing people's mistakes.

What I have to train my mind toward is encouraging others. Being critical is my problem. I do not natively think of and make encouragement my practice. Encouraging others is something I have to work at doing.

What you and I need to do is practice observing our friends and family members getting it right rather than getting it wrong. We need to exercise our getting it right muscle. If we do catch them getting it right, isolate and identify those moments. Those times are when God's grace is actively working in their lives.

We need to talk about what we saw and how encouraging it was to us. Remember, if you or I do anything right, it is evidence that God is working in our lives. If you are encouraging someone for getting it right, you are expressing your gratitude for the grace of God in their lives.

Encouragement Illustrated

When you observe someone getting it right, and you encourage them for what they did, it has a sevenfold effect:

1. They are encouraged in their behavior.

2. They gain insight as to how Jesus behaved.

3. They learn good and acceptable behaviors.

4. You both can praise God for His work in their lives.

5. The encouraged is built up in the faith.

6. You strengthen your relationship with them.

7. You have more liberty to bring critique to them.

Do you have a well-tuned, got-it-right antenna? As you might imagine, this approach takes more time and is harder to perfect than being a nitpicker. It takes more effort to catch people doing well, but when you do catch them getting it right, it motivates them toward change because it is God's kindness that leads to change.

Gospel Living Makes Confession Easier

God's kindness not only motivates you to change, but it motivates you to come to Him in your time of need. Because of the continued daily encouragement you receive through the gospel, you are aware that you can approach your Father, and He will not lash out at you, hurt you, or call you names. It is logical for you to assume He will be kind when you come to Him with your problems. He has shown His kindness in the past, and you can be assured He will be kind to you when you come to Him in the future.

One of the implications of the cross is how God will not give you what you deserve. He will not punish you for your sin. The Lord will deal kindly with you. He will help you change. Because of His prior kindness in salvation, you know there will be future kindness in sanctification. The kindness of God was not only effective in securing your salvation, but it is effective in your ongoing change needs.

1. Does the person you want to see change know you are for them? (cf. Romans 8:31) Do they understand when they come to you, they will be encouraged to change, rather than manipulated into change?

2. Are they aware you have their best interests in mind? (cf. Philippians 2:3–4) Are they motivated to come to you when they mess up because they know you will treat them like God treats you—with kindness?

3. Because of how you respond to them, are they motivated to be transparent with you about their problems?

Prior encouragement sets the stage for future grace in interactive relationships. Your past gospel experience informs you about your future experience with God. It will be a kind and gentle experience. You trust God to carefully and kindly care for your soul. And, of course, you want to imitate Him (Ephesians 5:1) as you gently and kindly help others change.

How are you doing in creating a context of grace in your relationships that motivates people to be honest, transparent, and willing to seek you out to receive your care?

Call to Action

1. Do you want someone to change?
2. Are you going to be nice, patient, and forbearing with them?
3. Are you going to motivate them to change with gospel strategies?
4. Are you going to treat them the way your heavenly Father treats you?

Let's Start Over

Here is how I began this chapter: Your friend needs to change. How do you help her change? Maybe your husband is stuck in a bad habit, and you want him to change. What is your change process? Perhaps your wife is nagging and criticizing. How are you helping her to model a more gentle and caring spirit? As you think about these questions in light of this chapter, how do you need to change?

Chapter 21

Being Intentionally Intrusive

Have you ever been hurt by someone? Have you ever been annoyed with someone? What about being disappointed or "put out" by the actions of another person? Yes, I know, these are silly questions. Of course, you have.

It happens to all of us. It does not matter where you go or what you do; a conflict will always be part of your life. The only way to successfully stay away from conflict is to stay away from people successfully, but even that will not work because of the personal war inside of you (James 4:1–3). Complete and uninterrupted shalom all the time is not possible with fallen people in a fallen world.

Social media has given rise to the avoidance and isolation method. Social media gives people a way to engage others while protecting themselves from being hurt by others. You can unfriend or unfollow someone with the click of a button.

At best, these cyber relationships are partial relationships. Even with our Internet advice to others, we can only hear their perspective. We cannot enter into their world, which is a core component of the gospel—Jesus came into our world.

We meet with our friends in cyberspace, always distant from them, limited in how we help them (Proverbs 18:17). The best way to help a person is to know them. The way you know them is to do authentic life in real time and space. Pulling away from real-life is also where counseling models have limitations.

Counseling at best is a limited context where the counselor is trying to know the real story of a person. Without entering into their narrative where

God is writing their story, the counselor will not be able to know them the way someone needs to know them. The counselor's help will be limited and short-term. Counseling offices and social media sites shield people from being fully known. Of course, this is why some people prefer these contexts.

1. The unwilling-to-change husband does not want anyone entering his real world, so he reluctantly goes to counseling.
2. The often-hurt person is afraid of letting people into her world, so she creates distance in cyberspace.

There are elements of intimacy and help in these contexts, but the intimacy is mostly false and the limitations circumvent the help because some of the essential pieces of soul care are not available. Things like transparency, honesty, vulnerability, and unmasked truth are not entirely accessible.

A New and Living Way

"Therefore, brothers, since we have confidence to enter the holy places by the blood of Jesus, by the new and living way that he opened for us through the curtain, that is, through his flesh, and since we have a great priest over the house of God, let us draw near with a true heart in full assurance of faith, with our hearts sprinkled clean from an evil conscience and our bodies washed with pure water. Let us hold fast the confession of our hope without wavering, for he who promised is faithful" (Hebrews 10:19–23).

The Bible calls you to live differently from superficial counseling or cyber relationships. The Bible calls you to be intentionally intrusive in people's lives so Jesus Christ can transform both of you. Though you have all the resources you need to be a better relationship-builder (2 Peter 1:3–4), there can be timidity about appropriating those things, which will keep you from enjoying the biblical, relational, and in-depth benefits you expect from the Christian family.

False intimacy begs the question, "Where do you begin to become a better relationship builder within God's family?" It starts with your relationship with Jesus. Your ability to persevere with others is tied directly to your relationship with God and how you appropriate His life into your life. A transformative relationship with the Lord will give you what you need to interact with any person regardless of how challenging it may be.

A key passage in understanding how to have strong biblical relationships is Hebrews 10:19–25. In the first part of the passage (Hebrews 10:19–23), the writer talks about how the right kind of life with Christ motivates and empowers you to have the right kind of life with others.

A synopsis of the first part of this passage could go like this: harmonic living with others is proportional to your appropriation of Christ (the gospel) into your life. If you are appropriately applying the gospel to your life, you will be ready to practically live it out in a community, which is the second part of the passage—how to live well with others.

Practically Considering Others

"And let us consider how to stir up one another to love and good works, not neglecting to meet together, as is the habit of some, but encouraging one another, and all the more as you see the Day drawing near" (Hebrews 10:24–25).

Before you can be in a right relationship with another person, you must first consider the other person. The word consider in this text means to become a student of the person in your life. Your goal is to exegete the person. You want to unpack them. You want to spend time thinking about them before you talk to them (James 1:19).

All good Christian disciplers know and practice this method of relationship-building. Even while a person is talking, you are actively listening to what they are saying. You're hearing what they are saying and not saying. You are discerning their presuppositions, worldview, categories, interpretative grid, and shaping influences. You are observing their words because you want to know what their actions reveal about their hearts (Luke 6:45).

That is how Jesus listened to people. He wanted to fully know what was in them (John 2:24–25) so that He could speak the true truth in love (Ephesians 4:15). You cannot help a person if you have not spent time considering them (1 Corinthians 1:4). A healthy Christian community is always considering each other. God has called you to consider how to help other people to be a better reflection of Jesus Christ.

1. Do you have people in your life who think about you?
2. Do you have people in your life who have given you permission to speak into their lives?
3. Are you doing life with other individuals who are committed to this kind of one another-ing?

Practically Confronting Others

The words stir up can also be translated spur, provoke, or even to irritate each other biblically. Yes. Irritate. The idea with irritating is not a sinful one, according to the context the Hebrew writer was writing. It is a command that means you are to be intentionally intrusive in other people's lives. If you have people around you who are not allowed to disagree with you, then you will not grow.

If you are too touchy, insecure, self-important, image conscious, or self-righteous, you are heading toward spiritual death. The sins that can most destroy you are the ones you cannot see. The most dangerous part of our sin problem is our blindness to our blindness.

The deceitfulness of sin causes us to minimize, rationalize, justify, and even not admit our sin. The mark of a mature Christian community is people who do not want to be blind to their sin. This kind of authenticity requires friends who are willing to go below the surface of each other's lives.

1. Have you given your friends permission to disagree with you?
2. Can your friends disagree with you without sinful reactions from you?
3. Are you willing to lovingly disagree with your friends for their good and God's glory?
4. Do you live in a community where intentional intrusive living is the norm?

Practically Comforting Others

The Greek word for comforting is parakaleo, which means to come alongside another person. Coming alongside another person is a critical thought in this text.

While you are confronting or correcting an individual in the context of spurring them on to love and good works, it is imperative for them to know you are for them. The "for them" aspect of any relationship is at the heart of the gospel. The main reason any Christian is willing to receive the Lord's corrective care is that he knows God is for him (Romans 5:8, 8:31; Hebrews 12:6).

It is unwise, unbiblical, and unkind to correct any person you are not for, which does not mean you are for their sin. You can be for a person but not for their sin. If you do not get this right in your heart and delivery, your corrective care may come across as punitive rather than redemptive.

The most important practice in bringing restorative care is prayer. If you have not spent time praying for and about the person, then your correction of that person may have a sinful edge to it.

In such cases, your care will come across as harsh or unkind. If you have spent time before the Father, bringing the annoying people in your life to Him, while pleading with Him to adjust your attitude, thoughts, words, and actions toward them, you will build them up, not tear them down (Ephesians 4:29).

"Blessed be the God and Father of our Lord Jesus Christ, the Father of mercies and God of all comfort, who comforts us in all our affliction, so that we may be able to comfort those who are in any affliction, with the comfort with which we ourselves are comforted by God" (2 Corinthians 1:3–4).

1. How often do you pray for those you need to correct?
2. Do those you biblically irritate feel your affection for them?
3. Could those you bring correction to make a case for how you are for them?

I Need Thee – Every Hour I Need Thee

You cannot draw near to God on our own. You need a community to spur you on to change. The author of Hebrews knew the dire straits his readers were in, which is why he used strong language to motivate them toward love and good works. People were murdering them.

His twofold aim in this text was to elevate the power of the gospel while giving them practical instruction on how to mobilize as a community to strengthen each other. If you are not accessing the community of faith while seeking to have that community know you the way you need to be known, your sanctification is in danger of shipwrecking. There is no biblical argument otherwise.

We have all been hurt by people, especially other Christians. Yes, we do shoot each other, don't we? Nevertheless, this does not negate the truth of this passage or the need for total, immersive, body ministry. I need people in my life who are willing to love me enough to bring corrective care to me. I am aware they will love me imperfectly, which is why I must know they are for me.

I can receive their imperfect care if they have demonstrated through their comforting encouragement that they are on my side. I am not asking my friends to agree with me, to turn a blind eye to my sin, or to coddle me. I am asking them to love God enough to where they will be motivated to be used by Him to speak into my life, especially in areas where I am self-deceived. There is safety in this kind of community, and we must not be satisfied until we are living in it.

Call to Action

1. Do you live in this kind of community?
2. What do you need to do to either create or sustain this sort of community?
3. How does being hurt by others hinder you from engaging others in a real community?
4. Will you find someone to help you work through your disappointments so that you can participate in a loving, intrusive community?
5. Will you work through all the questions in this chapter with a friend while asking the Father to bring to light anything that keeps you from this kind of community?

Chapter 22

An Unchangeable Situation

Biff and Mable have been struggling in their marriage for a long time. Biff gets quiet, and Mable gets loud. This method is their standard endless loop of perpetuated interaction. After years of trying and failing, they lost hope that things would ever change. As a last-ditch effort, they came to counseling. Though their hearts were not in the counseling, they were willing to give it a try.

Biff wanted Mable to change while Mable was frustrated how Biff's ability to change moved at the speed of a tortoise. She got mad. He was mentally disengaged. The beat went on.

Collision Course

After listening to them talk (argue), posture for personal rights, and critique each other for a while, I finally told Mable her plan was not working and recommended a new one. I described her plan as something like two trains headed toward each other at full throttle. They collide. My train illustration is her getting mad and Biff getting quiet.

Her anger does not mean she is the blame more than Biff. It does not matter who deserves the most blame. The main thing, at least at this point, is addressing their personal stubbornness and anger. After the trains collide, they go back to their separate stations, and in a day or two, they restart their engines only to run full throttle into each other again. They have been going through this routine for over a decade.

Interestingly, Mable has read a half of a dozen books on overcoming anger while Biff has done little to change the spiritual climate in their home. I told Mable the first place to start is to stop reading all those how to overcome anger, how to jump-start your marriage books. They are not going to work for her. The problem is not primarily her anger or failing marriage. It's her expectation for a different kind of marriage.

As long as she thinks her situation must change, the more she will build up a head of steam and run full throttle into her husband. Result: He will sulk, she will stew, and they both will do it all over again tomorrow.

1. Her marriage is a problem.
2. Her passive husband is a problem.
3. Her anger is a problem.

But all three of those things are sustained and perpetuated by her expectation (and even demand) for something different. Her expectations do not place the blame on her. My appeal is for them to think about how expectations, no matter how aligned they may be with the Bible's teachings, can derail your heart.

Just because you want what the Bible teaches, it does not mean you will get it. Jesus wanted to live. That was not the narrative His Father had in mind. There are two ditches you must avoid:

1. I will have what I want, especially when the Bible does not forbid my desires.
2. I will resign myself to a pitiful life because God is not giving me the desires of my heart.

In between those two ditches is a practical faith that allows you to be a "man of sorrows, acquainted with grief" (Isaiah 53:3) while entrusting yourself to Him who judges justly (2 Peter 2:20–25). The only way to find that sweet spot is through the door of death (Hebrews 2:14–15; Luke 14:26–27).

Unchanging Problems

I told her how things would be easier to understand and accept if she was in a car wreck and relegated to a wheelchair for the rest of her life. A person receiving bad news of this nature would eventually realize how their situation is unchangeable. It is "easier" to get over the disappointment that is final than it is to get over the disappointment of something that could change.

The problem with Mable is she expects her husband to be a spiritual leader. She expects him to be nice, to love her like Christ, and to rear their children in the nurture and admonition of the Lord (Ephesians 6:4). She expects him to set the spiritual tone in the home by fighting sin while modeling Jesus (Ephesians 5:1). She expects to have a Christ-centered home.

Can you see how she has set herself up for disappointment, anger, and possible bitterness? The longer she clings to her expectations, the deeper she will find herself in the slough of despond. It reminds me of Paul "counseling" the Corinthian church. He knew he couldn't overfocus on how they were messing things up while doggedly expecting them to change into God-glorifying, gospel-focused, others-centered Christians. It's like a few counseling sessions I have had.

If I become bound to the expectation that a person's change into Christlikeness is the only thing that will make me happy, I am going to be in deep emotional weeds. The temptation to sin against them would be inevitable, and my disappointment would only grow.

I have learned—somewhat imperfectly—that I am not called to change people. I am called to love God and others while not hanging emotionally charged expectations on their change (1 Corinthians 3:6). And yes, I'm aware it's easier for me to be this way with people that I don't live with, but you need to know I do live with individuals who do not always meet my expectations or timeframes.

God did not promise I would receive everything I desired, when I desired it, and how I desired it. In fact, He promised something entirely the opposite. He promised a boatload of problems. Not just one boatload but many. (See

Genesis 3:14, 3:16, and 3:17–18.) You will know if you have forgotten about the Christian's thorn and thistle theology by how you respond to the personal suffering that comes into your life. Both Biff and Mable were resisting this aspect of their death walk with Christ (Luke 9:23).

If God would write "execute my Son" into the story of Christ's life, do you think it is out of the realm of possibility that He might write something into your life that you might not like (Isaiah 53:10; Luke 22:42)? Whenever you sin, whether it is the anger of silent treatment (Biff) or the anger of loudness (Mable), you are revealing your thoughts about the Author of your story.

They are focusing too much on the things they can see in their horizontal world with each other. And they are not factoring in the things they cannot see in their vertical world with God.

Biff and Mable were eaten up with and ticked off by what they could see. Biff had lost hope that things would change, so he kept to himself. Mable had lost hope that things would change, so she yelled at Biff. Think again about the two trains on an inevitable head-on collision course. Now think about it repeatedly happening for over a decade. Would you lose hope? I would.

Losing Heart

"So we do not lose heart. Though our outer nature is wasting away, our inner nature is being renewed day by day. For this slight momentary affliction is preparing for us an eternal weight of glory beyond all comparison, as we look not to the things that are seen but to the things that are unseen. For the things that are seen are transient, but the things that are unseen are eternal" (2 Corinthians 4:16–18).

Biff and Mable have lost heart. They are looking at the outer nature of things—the things they can see, the things that are unchangeable, the things that are wasting away. They realize how they can't fix the other person or their marriage. For them, it is not so much about their bodies as Paul was referring to, as it is about the wasting away of their marriage and family. Each time they take a survey of their home life, they become discouraged (or angry).

They have habituated themselves into extreme negativity. Just one look at what Biff and Mable can see and the two trains take off toward each other. Because of their fixation on what they want, neither one of them will be satisfied until they get it. Thus, they choose to bite and devour each other (Galatians 5:15).

Unsee-able Seeing

Think through some of the Bible characters and reimagine what their lives would have been like if they responded to their problems like Biff and Mable.

"For time would fail me to tell of Gideon, Barak, Samson, Jephthah, of David and Samuel and the prophets—who through faith conquered kingdoms, enforced justice, obtained promises, stopped the mouths of lions, quenched the power of fire, escaped the edge of the sword, were made strong out of weakness, became mighty in war, put foreign armies to flight. Women received back their dead by resurrection. Some were tortured, refusing to accept release, so that they might rise again to a better life. Others suffered mocking and flogging, and even chains and imprisonment. They were stoned, they were sawn in two, they were killed with the sword. They went about in skins of sheep and goats, destitute, afflicted, mistreated—of whom the world was not worthy— wandering about in deserts and mountains, and in dens and caves of the earth" (Hebrews 11:32–38).

Take note of a few ideas that describe their worldview and compare them to how you think about the hardships that are happening to you.

1. They accomplished impossible things through faith.
2. They were made strong out of weakness.

3. They knew they were going to rise to a better life.

4. They did not see the world as being worthy.

Their predecessor, Moses, responded similarly to the life-altering events the Lord wrote into his story. Take a look at how he thought about and responded to his unchangeable situation.

"By faith he left Egypt, not being afraid of the anger of the king, for he endured as seeing him who is invisible" (Hebrews 11:27).

The only way Biff and Mable are going to endure is if they make a real, volitional, and practical decision to take their eyes off what they can see and choose to keep their eyes on whom they cannot see. If Biff and Mable do not realign their sights to something more eternal—their great, invisible God, they will continue to spiral into relational dysfunction and conflict. Their marriage will not be able to sustain many more of these train collisions.

God's Opposition

For the record, the collision they keep having with each other is not really about running into another train at all. It is the hand of God that stands in opposition to both of them (James 4:6). If there is any hope for their unchangeable situation changing, one or both of them will have to change tracks by doing things God's way.

Sinful methods will never gain the favor of God. Warning: It may not be God's will to change your spouse (2 Corinthians 12:7–10; Deuteronomy 29:29). Every person does not pursue righteousness (Revelation 20:15).

Though you know this theological warning and probably do not struggle with it in theory, you will be challenged at the deepest level of your soul if the unchanging person is in your life. It is within the realm of possibility for the Lord to use an imperfect marriage for purposes you cannot perceive right now.

"Three times I pleaded with the Lord about this, that it should leave me. But he said to me, 'My grace is sufficient for you, for my power is made perfect in weakness.' Therefore I will boast all the more gladly of my weaknesses, so that the power of Christ may rest upon me. For the sake of Christ, then, I am content with weaknesses, insults, hardships, persecutions, and calamities. For when I am weak, then I am strong" (2 Corinthians 12:8–10).

If you are in a miserable marriage, your first call to action is to fight for contentment in your soul before you engage your spouse to change. The hardest battle you will ever fight is a "God plus nothing" life experience.

Call to Action

1. What Can You Do? – James said if you know what to do but do not do it, then it is a sin (James 4:17). With that in mind, is there something you need to do in your marriage that could make it better? How do you need to change to put Christ on display in your marriage?

2. What Are Your Motives? – While a good motivation is to improve your marriage, your first and most important motive must be to glorify God regardless of the outcome (1 Corinthians 10:31). You will know if your primary motive is about changing your marriage or glorifying God by how you respond when someone does not meet your expectations.

3. How Do You Respond? – When you do the right thing in your marriage, but the results are disappointing, how do you respond? If you respond poorly, how do you need to change?

4. Take Your Thoughts Captive – As you think about the possibility of your situation never changing, what goes through your mind? How is God meeting you while you're not getting what you want from Him or your relationship?

5. Do Not Do This Alone – God made you for a community. Your marriage is your first community. Then comes your church. If your marriage "community" is not helping you, reach out to your church family. Let them help you.

Chapter 23

Most Perfect Relationship

You are a relational being because God created you in His image (Genesis 1:26). God, who has always belonged to a community—a Trinitarian community, made you in such a way that you want to belong to a community (Genesis 2:18). It is impossible for the Lord to create anything that is not affected by Him: His fingerprints are all over His work. You see this idea in Romans 1:20 where Paul talked about how the non-regenerate person could learn about God through His creation. You can see clearly God's invisible attributes through the world He created.

Made in the image of God means, in part, that you have similarities to God (James 3:9). One of the most intrinsic qualities He put into you is a desire to commune with others—those who are like you. To want to relate to other people is God-like; it is imaging the Trinity.

A reason the Lord created Eve was so that Adam could more adequately image his Creator. Without an object to receive his love, Adam would not be able to know, experience, or emulate God entirely. Talking about ice cream and tasting ice cream are two different things. Adam could know about love, but he could not fully experience love until he tasted it (Psalm 34:8), until he could do what God was doing: loving another person (1 John 4:8).

As they say, "You cannot understand a person until you walk a mile in their shoes." Adam could not "walk a mile in the Lord's shoes" because he had no person like him to walk in similar paths. Without Eve, Adam's life would have a dead-end street feel to it. Your life would be similar if you were not communing within a community. One of the most extreme expressions of this is solitary confinement.

The Lord saw this problem and said it was not good for Adam to be alone (Genesis 2:18), so He gave Adam a friend. For the first time in the history of the human race, Adam could live out a fuller reflection of his Creator by having an object for his affection. Then you turn the page.

Along Came Sin

In Genesis chapter three you are introduced to sin through a walking, talking, stalking serpent. You know the story. Adam and Eve chose to sin, and from that point forward every person born from them was selfish (Romans 5:12).

The love Adam was supposed to give to Eve turned onto himself. Eve reciprocated with a similar kind of self-centered love. Rather than seeing the other person as an opportunity to image God through others-centered loving, our first two parents became self-serving.

Adam and Eve replaced esteeming others more than themselves with esteeming themselves more than others, or what we call self-esteem today (Philippians 2:3–4). Selfishness is how sin transforms you. The Father, knowing that selfish people could never save selfish people, sent His others-centered Son to reverse the curse (Ephesians 2:1–10).

Now, the gospel gives you an opportunity for a second birth (John 3:7), so you can be reequipped, reenvisioned, and rerouted for how things are supposed to be. Even though the God-centered community was interrupted by the fall, the possibility of enjoying an others-centered community is available to anyone who wants it.

True Community

The purest iteration of this kind of community is the Father, Son, and Spirit. They are perfect koinonia. There is nothing more refined, more exquisite, and more profound than Father, Son, and Spirit. If you want to enjoy the most perfect human relationship possible, the Trinity has to be part of that relationship.

Any human relationship without God is less than what it could be or should be. That is why non-Christians cannot have true koinonia. The Spirit will not inhabit the natural person (1 Corinthians 2:14). Paul hinted at this in Philippians 2:1 when he talked about participation in the Spirit.

The word participation is the word koinonia or the word community. To have a true community with another human being, both persons must enter into a mutual, reciprocating, and effective participation (fellowship) in the Spirit. A husband and wife can relate to each other well and have many wonderful experiences together, but there will always be something missing in their relationship if they are not sharing their transparent and transcendent relationship with God with each other.

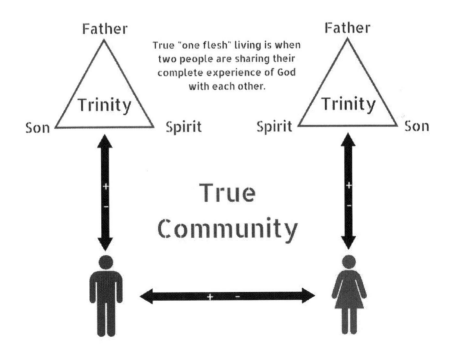

If they are not participating together with the Spirit of God, even if they have enjoyed every possible human experience, they will never fully experience the koinonia the Lord generously provides to any two (or more) people who want to participate with Him in that kind of community.

Unpacking Community

Biblical fellowship—participation in the Spirit or community—means the sharing with another individual your deepest and richest relationship, which is your relationship with God.

Think about the most powerful and profound relationship you can have; it is with God, of course. There is no other relationship better than what you have with the Lord. How could anything be better than the King of the universe, the Person who created you and sustains you, communing with you?

That means if you want to have the most robust, profound, off-the-charts, relationship with another human being, your call to action is to share with that person your experience with sovereign Creator, King—the Lord God Almighty. If you do, you will be sharing with another individual your greatest treasure (Matthew 6:21).

To let another person in on your greatest treasure is the most vulnerable, intimate, profound, rich, transcending, honest, transparent, and complimenting thing you could do for a relationship. The infographic helps to unpack what it means to have biblical fellowship with another person. Of course, true community applies to any friendship, e.g., if your small group could do this, you would belong to one of the richest groups in the world.

The man in the infographic could be anyone. I am going to call him Rick. The woman we will call Lucia. You can see that Rick and Lucia have an individualized, independent, and personal relationship with God.

Rick and Lucia are enjoying the deepest kind of relationship a person could ever enjoy. They both are participating in the Spirit; the Lord has inhabited them. They are empowered, illuminated, encouraged, and motivated by God, as well as convicted and made to feel guilty when they sin against God (Proverbs 3:12; Hebrews 12:6).

Rick and Lucia have a full relationship with the Lord, which includes all their good and bad days. There are things they are doing well in their walk with God (Ephesians 4:1), and there are things they have not fully matured into yet (Hebrews 5:12–14).

On the positive side of things: Rick and Lucia are appropriating the grace of God in their lives, and they are enjoying biblical success with God and each other (Joshua 1:8). On the downside of things: Rick and Lucia are not appropriating the grace of God in all ways in their lives, and the Spirit of God is grieved or quenched at times (Ephesians 4:30; 1 Thessalonians 5:19).

Rick and Lucia are representative of all Christians. You could say they have a light and a dark side (1 John 1:7–10) regarding their walk with the Lord. The right and wrong of their whole selves represent the totality of how they do community (koinonia) with the Lord.

Human Koinonia

Being married and being a Christian does not automatically mean you will connect and relate to your spouse at the deepest part of your personal experience, which is your intimate knowledge of and experience with God. You could go to church for years and never enjoy biblical fellowship with your spouse or any other person. Though you have to be a Christian to experience this kind of community, being a Christian does not automatically mean you have it.

That sort of community requires a deeper amount of trust to engage another person in the deepest part of the soul. Maybe you could reflect on it as you might think about those who babysit your children (if you have kids). You would not give your most cherished treasure to someone whom you do not trust. If the person you are sharing your deepest treasure with cannot steward the high honor of receiving your best treasure, you must disqualify them from entering into that experience with you.

As it relates to your relationship with the Lord, you may share part of your experience with Him with your spouse. You may let your spouse know some of the things you are learning or some of the ways you think about God and life. But if your spouse has a proven record of not being able to steward your deepest secrets, the deeper things will continue to be between you and the Lord. There is a level of koinonia you will not go to with your spouse or with any other friend if they are not mature enough to handle the full truth about you (John 16:12).

"There is therefore now no condemnation for those who are in Christ Jesus" (Romans 8:1).

There are many things you and I appreciate about the Lord, but probably nothing ranks higher than the fact that He does not condemn us. There is no more condemnation toward those who have been saved by our Redeemer. All of our past, present, and future sins are under the blood of Christ, blotted out forever, and never held against us in any divine court of law. We have been justified, set free, declared not guilty, and as long as Christ lives, we will live in that freedom (Galatians 5:1). That truth has set us free (John 8:36).

It sets us free to enter into His courts (Psalm 100:4), ready to share all of the thoughts and intentions of our hearts with Him, even though He already knows them (Hebrews 4:12–13). We do this because we are not afraid of Him. We are aware He is for us (Romans 8:31–39). We can be naked before God and not ashamed (Genesis 2:25).

What I am describing is the kind of relationship every married couple should be pursuing with each other. This kind of koinonia will not happen in a year or a decade but in a lifetime of pressing into God and each other. Sharing the farthest depths of our experience with God should be the goal for every couple.

One Thing Thou Lackest

It is typical when people come to me for counseling to talk about how they are having communication problems. I do not think many (if any of them) understand all the necessary contours of that word. Communication comes from the Greek word koinonia. I think that if they fully understood the depth of their communication problems, they would be more discouraged.

What they are typically talking about and asking for are talk tips, some practical advice to help them communicate well with each other. I understand. They are trying to get along with each other, but they do not clearly know how they are a million miles from what the Bible talks about when it talks about getting along with someone.

Christ did not come just to help us to get along with each other. He came to transform us into Himself (1 John 3:8). In heaven, there will be perfect koinonia because there will be no sin. On earth, we have to fight for this kind of communication in relationships. There is a high price to pay to be able to enjoy communal participation in the Spirit.

The biggest hindrance to koinonia is that we do not trust each other to handle the real truth about our lives. So, what do we do? We do not go there with them. I remember in the early part of our marriage how Lucia would share certain things with her friends—things she had not shared with me.

I would become angry each time she did this. It was an insult. It was an affront. I would reason, "Why does she share her more intimate and personal thoughts with other people, but not with me?" My first response was to become angry with her. It took a long time for me to realize how my jerk-ness was intimidating her from being intimate with me. It did not occur to me that the reason she would not share with me was that I was not mature enough to handle her truth.

She knew she could share her deeper struggles with others, but she could not share those things with me because I was not trustworthy. Because of how I had responded to her in the past, she felt it would be wiser and safer not to let me into the deeper places of her heart.

- It takes a lot of courage for a person to share their struggles with someone.
- It takes a lot of other-loving maturity to steward those deeper matters of the heart.

Call to Action

1. Are you currently experiencing true community with your closest friend? If you are married, that friend should be your spouse.
2. If you are not, what is hindering you? Make this question about you, not about the other person. Key verse: Matthew 7:3–5.
3. What are three practical things you can do to begin to have a deeper participation with your friend?

Chapter 24

Leading Your Wife in Conversations

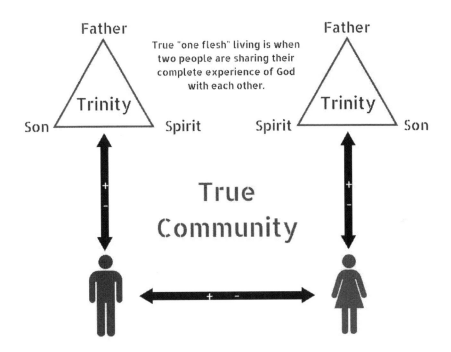

To fully release your vulnerable and intimate soul to another person, you must know the person is trustworthy and will lovingly steward all of your inner truth. This quality in a marriage is one of the most important leadership requirements for a husband to lead his wife.

You build your strongest and deepest relationships upon trust, which is why you love God so much. Trust is also why you share with Him your deepest and darkest thoughts. He will never condemn you. (See Romans 8:1.)

And, this is why you are okay with His corrective care when you sin—you know He loves you (Hebrews 12:6). His corrections flow out of His unending and unstoppable love for you. This kind of love gives Him an all-access pass into your life. He is the unique and perfect example to follow when it comes to relationship making. He is the person you want to emulate.

It took me a while to understand this when it came to our marriage because I did not fully realize the importance of the "for us clause" in the gospel. In Romans 8:31 Paul asked, "If God is for us, who could be against us?" Then he went on to explain what being "for us" meant as he doxologized about the gospel:

"He, who did not spare his own Son but gave him up for us all, how will he not also with him graciously give us all things?" (Romans 8:32).

Do you see what Paul did? He connected how the Lord is for you to a practical outworking of the gospel. He said the Lord was for you, and he proved his point by reminding you that He sent His one and only Son to die on a cross to save you.

But what does it mean to me?

If a person is willing to die for you, then you can rest assured he is for you. He loves you with an inexhaustible love (John 15:13). And if he is for you to that degree, you know he can be trusted—the essential requirement to release your vulnerable soul to another person fully.

This kind of gospel connection to your everyday life is not what I was demonstrating to my wife in the early years of our marriage. Though I was not a tyrant, and though we had many great times together, I was not fully and practically in tune with what it meant to be a gospelized man.

Yes, I was for her in the sense that nobody else could mess with her, but I was not for her in the way the Lord is for me. This gospel lack in my life was enough to give her pause when it came to sharing her innermost thoughts and struggles with me. What I am saying is I was not trustworthy to the degree I needed to be to release her from fear, while inviting her to share with me in an open and vulnerable way. I had left just enough questions in her mind to make her wary of letting me fully into her world.

Flying Without a Sin Plan

When we were dating, there was hardly a thing we did not discuss. It was open season on conversation, and all doors flung wide open as we shared our dreams as well as our fears. The love flowed in those early days of dating. We had not known each other long enough to become disappointed or discouraged with each other. Sin was present, but it had not affected us enough to shut us down relationally.

That came later.

After we tied the knot and entered into a 24/7 relationship, the doctrine of sin began to become more of an issue. We were ignorant; we were two young people in love with no sin plan.

Because we could not get away from each other, we could no longer keep our sinful ways masked from each other. And not being trained in how to wage war biblically, we waged war according to the flesh (2 Corinthians 10:3). I've listed a few of our first fighting characteristics—some of the tools that made up our poor fighting techniques.

Justification	Anger	Frustration	Excusing
Self-righteous	Condemnation	Guilt	Grumbling
Accusing	No Confession	Rationalization	Shame
Criticalness	Selfishness	Silence	Manipulation
Blame	Arrogance	Pouting	Unforgiveness

Any of these characteristics will create distance in a relationship, with no possibility of having biblical koinonia. And to further complicate matters was my unwillingness to own the sins I committed in the marriage. That is where we were.

Religious But Distant

On the surface, we went to church. We did ministry things. We prayed and read our Bibles every day. We were religious people in the proper sense of that word. But there was a distance between us.

We both had independent relationships with the Lord—relationships that did not intersect with each other. It is possible we could have made it to the end of our lives and still be together, still be in church, and still doing ministry things in some way, shape, or form. I do not think those external activities would have changed a lot, even though our spiritual lives were like two ships passing in the night. There was no connection at the deepest and richest parts of our lives.

How sad when you are not able to share your most treasured experience with the person you married: the Lord is an amazing gift but not mutually enjoyed. Like a couple sitting in bed, playing video games on their own devices with people around the world, but not playing with each other. I shared my experience with God with others, and Lucia shared her experience with God with others, but we did not have a shared experience with God with each other.

The depth of our God-talk with each other was to talk about churchy things and churchy people. We could not connect at the soul level. When it came to each other, we lived happily on the outside but spiritually lonely on the inside.

From Insult to Owning

Initially, I was offended that she would have spiritually intimate relationships with other people, but as the Lord began to open my eyes, I began to see how I had set the tone for that kind of environment in our home. She did not shut down like that at the beginning of our relationship. She was open with me and longed for me to lead her into more openness. Of course, I had no clue about such matters, so when she disappointed me, I responded with various forms of anger, i.e., harsh words, silent treatment, and accusation.

I did not realize how my insensitivity was perpetuating a darkness in our home. Each unkind word was like a paper cut on her heart. Rather than owning my unkindness, I continued to wax on with my eye-for-an-eye responses to her (Matthew 7:3–5, 5:38–48).

Most Christian women want to be loved and led well (1 Peter 3:7). They want to be vulnerable (Ephesians 5:29). I have described it to many couples like a person walking up to you with their heart in their hands, reaching it out to give to you. Imagine standing there with another person's beating heart in your hands. That is the fragility we live before the Lord, knowing He could stomp us out in a moment. Yet we are willing to come before Him in that kind of vulnerability because we trust Him.

A wife will never do that with her husband if he has a proven track record of not being trusted with the high honor of stewarding her heart. That is what finally dawned on me. That is what I began to own. I had not created an environment of grace in our marriage. We were physically intimate. We loved each other. We continued to do a lot of fun things together, but there was a no trespassing sign on her heart, and I was the one who put it there.

Step One: Step Up

Biblical fellowship is sharing with another human your deepest and richest relationship, which is your relationship with God. There are two parts to that relationship—a good and bad side, or a light and dark side. There are positive aspects in your life where you are appropriating the Lord's grace and living in the strength of His victory through the resurrection. Then there are other areas in your life where you have not appropriated the Lord's grace, and you are struggling.

Biblical fellowship with another human being is when both people can share both sides of their experience with the Lord—the good and the bad side. The key to living in this kind of fellowship is trust: can I trust you to steward my deepest vulnerabilities?

It became apparent to me that if I wanted to get into the deepest part of Lucia's soul, I needed to lead her by being vulnerable to her. I needed to step up to the plate and lead her in biblical koinonia, rather than waiting for her to lead me. It was time to let her in on my dirty little secret: I was a failure as a husband. The irony is that she was well-aware of my dirty little secret. The bigger obstacle was my unwillingness to own my failure, which only affirmed to her that I could not be trusted.

If a man is a thief but will not own his thievery, you know you cannot trust him. It is one thing to steal, but to steal and not own your stealing makes you a person that others will have to be doubly cautious with when engaging. A person who will not own his sin has trustworthy issues, not to mention integrity, honesty, transparency, deception, self-righteousness, controlling, and discernment problems. Shall I go on with more reasons that caused Lucia pause in her soul when it came to opening up to me?

As the leader of my home, it was my call as to whether I was going to make the first move. It was my overbearingness that put her on her heels, and it would be the empowering grace of God working through humility that would begin to build the faith she needed to trust me again.

In the past, I would wait for her to open up and own her sin. In those moments, I could fake humility while feeling smug, self-righteous, and grateful that she agreed with me. Think about how punishing that had to feel to her.

1. Lucia sins.

2. Lucia leads by owning her sin.

3. Then I further condemn her through my arrogance and self-righteousness as I pontificate about her sin and how she needs to change.

Step Two: Live the Gospel

I honestly wanted Lucia to share with me her deepest thoughts. I did not want her only to find safety with others. It took me the longest time to realize if that is what I wanted, I needed to lead her into it.

Getting her to open up was not going to happen by verbally beating it out of her. Manipulating her through well-thought-out arguments, as though communication was a competitive event, was not going to work either.

And as for critique and shame? Forget about it. The radicality of the gospel cuts against the grain of prideful men. Here are a few examples that speak to that radicality:

1. The way up is down (Philippians 2:1–11).

2. The way in is out (Hebrews 13:13).

3. The first will be last (Matthew 20:16).

4. Life comes through death (John 12:24).

5. Man's wisdom is foolish, and God's foolishness is wisdom (1 Corinthians 1:18–25).

6. To be strong, you must be weak (2 Corinthians 12:10).

7. And if a man is going to lead his wife, he will have to learn how to serve her (Mark 10:45).

If koinonia is the goal, open the door of your heart and invite her to your authentic self. Give her a tour. Do a walk-through, articulating your failures, fears, and weaknesses. Let her see and experience your vulnerability.

Call to Action

Here are five questions you can share with your wife—a suggestive way for you to consider how to approach this type of communication in your marriage. If this kind of communication has not been the norm for you both, you may want to preface the questions with the following:

Honey, if you knew I would not defend myself in any way or retaliate in any way, how would you respond to the following things? You are completely free to answer in any way you want to, and I will not defend myself, correct you, or try to manipulate you to my way of thinking. I also will not bring this conversation up in the future in a punitive way. My hope is for you to experience the grace of God through my example, so it will release you to help me in areas where I have failed.

Do not say that if you don't mean it. These words are not a technique. If you have a change of heart and your words are true, here are a few biblical fellowship starter questions as you share your thoughts about yourself with your wife while drawing her out to give input. (Consider this your starter pack.)

1. What is an area of your life, husband, where you regularly fail and cannot gain victory? Talk to your wife about this area, leading her to a conversation, while asking her for help.

2. What is one way you have failed her? Talk to her about this, seeking her forgiveness and asking how you can more effectively serve her.

3. What is a fear you have? Share that fear with your wife. You hold your heart in your hands while reaching it out for her loving stewardship.

4. Ask your wife to give her perspective on one of your blind spots—a thing you may not be able to see. Draw her out, appealing to her to help you see what you cannot see.

5. Ask your wife if she feels like you are for her (Romans 8:31). Draw her out by using specifics.

Chapter 25

Build and Enjoy Community Life

The most important relationship in your life is with God. And the most practical way to experience Him is in a community of like-minded believers who are intentional about helping each other mature in their relationships with Him.

To know God better means your primary relationships should provide you contexts to deepen your experience with Him (1 Corinthians 10:31). If your primary relationships do not give you that kind of care, you should consider changing your closest network of friends (Matthew 5:30; Hebrews 12:1).

While it is true that bad companions can corrupt your morals (1 Corinthians 15:33), it is also true that good companions can make you a better person. Good friends is a solid reason you should pursue biblical companions —those who want to motivate you to live a God-glorifying life (Hebrews 10:24–25).

1. Would you characterize your relationships as good or bad companions?
2. Is your boyfriend (or girlfriend) a good companion?
3. What about your spouse?

If your closest relationships are not spurring you on to love God more effectively, you should reconsider how you do life with them.

The What

Your life experience with God is the prize (Philippians 3:12–14). It is your hope to be progressively changed into Christlikeness (2 Corinthians 3:18) so that you can enjoy a fuller experience with Him. The Lord is the "what" when it comes to building a community of friends.

215

"What" do you want to do? Experience the Lord in more profound ways. With the Lord clearly established as the goal, you begin developing a methodology that will allow you to fulfill your call to walk in a manner that is worthy of the calling He has placed on your life (Ephesians 4:1–3, 5:1–2).

This methodology is the "how" part of experiencing God. The "how" makes the word koinonia an important word. It is the word for community, fellowship, and participation. (See other koinonia verses in Philippians 1:5, 2:1; 1 Corinthians 1:9; 1 John 1:3, 6–7.)

To fully experience God, there must be a community of like-minded people who are willing to participate in the Spirit for the cause of biblical fellowship. It is not possible to know the Lord in all the ways you can know Him without body-to-body reciprocality. (See 1 Corinthians 12:27; Matthew 25:44–45.)

- The "what" of community life is to deepen your experience with God.
- The "how" of community life is to build relationships that want to deepen their mutual experiences with the Lord.

The How

With the Lord as the goal for your community, you can now begin delving into the practical aspects of building and knitting your lives together. Here are seven suggestions for you to think about as you create a richer community life experience.

1. Establish Your Goal

I will not develop this any further than what I have already mentioned but will only reiterate the importance of making the Lord the prize for doing community life. If deepening your experience with God is not your chief purpose, your community will deteriorate into a social club.

If you think about your primary relationships in a "mission statement" way, this could be your Community Mission Statement: "We are here to deepen our relationship with the Lord, which will happen in proportion to which we deepen our relationship with each other."

---

2. Understand Koinonia

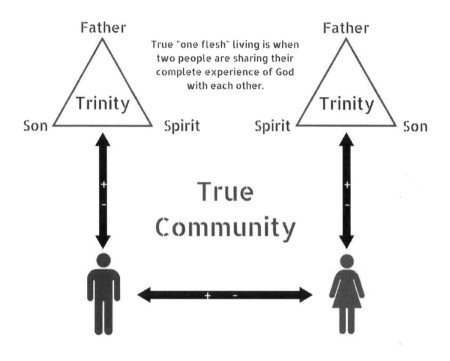

Each person in your community will have to decide if they are going to share their complete experience with God with each other authentically. There are good and bad sides to how they relate to God. For example, there are areas in their lives where they are not appropriating the grace of God, as evidenced by personal struggles and inter-relational conflict. Nobody is perfect. Everyone is a work-in-progress.

Everybody in your group of close friends will have sin problems and patterns in their lives. There are no exceptions to this rule. It will be easier to share how they are experiencing victory in Jesus, but it will be a struggle for them to be self-disclosing in areas where they are not experiencing that success.

The proportion in which every person in your community is self-disclosing will be the proportion in which your community will experience their fullest possibilities with God. Nothing in group life will be harder than living out this truth. It is impossible to enjoy a complete expression of koinonia if your closest friends are not willing to share their entire experience with God. The same holds true for you.

Sharing half-truths about how you are doing with the Lord will only allow others to enter into half of your experience with the Lord—the safe side, where you are living the dream. However, if you don't let them into the darker side of your life, there is a good chance you will always remain there.

3. Model Your Mission

Because you do not want to be naked and ashamed (Genesis 2:25), you cover yourself with fig leaves. That is what Adamic people do. You carry a sense of fear, shame, and guilt, and you hope no one will expose you for who you are. The most effective way to motivate a person to share their complete experience with the Lord, specifically the darker side of themselves, is for you to share areas in which you are struggling. You become the model for the kind of person you want them to be.

All good counselors know this truth. When someone comes to counseling, the counselee can easily (and wrongly) assume the counselor has his act together. This presumption can intimidate the counselee and even hinder him from being self-disclosing.

A wise counselor will want to diffuse this wrongheaded notion by letting the counselee know that he—the counselor—does not have it all together. There have been many times in counseling where I have shared my sin struggles. My hope in doing so is to release the person from being fearful about being transparent. Trying to hide your sin is as futile as trying to hide your skin color.

The quicker you can get over yourself, the faster you can access one of the most effective means of grace given to you: the body of Christ. A wise, humble, and community-minded person will openly talk about the good and bad side of his relationship with the Lord.

4. Build Trust

The thing that will hinder you from openly sharing the darker things in your life is trust. "Can I trust you?" Usually, trust issues revolve around two important questions:

- How will you respond to me after I reveal the real me? Will you judge me? Will you make fun of me? Will you critique me or gossip about me?
- Are you competent enough to help me? If I do share my struggles with you, are you able to help me?

This relational tension is where you will need to be patient with people (1 Thessalonians 5:14). It can take years for someone to open up. Sanctification may sound nice on paper, but when you put a bunch of messed up people in a room together, things can become quite complicated.

5. Enjoy Small Talk

Because of the tentativeness of people, it will be important for you to learn the value of small talk. Small talk leads to deep talk. Typically, it is unwise to launch into deep conversations with people you do not know. It is even more unwise to pull things out of people—those who are not comfortable with that kind of intrusive conversation. They may want help at some level, but they have to come to you on their terms, not yours.

Do not expect in six weeks of relationship building with a friend what you have learned in twenty years of walking with the Lord. Give it time. Love on your friends while encouraging them and building trust. You keep on modeling your mission. Let them see your freedom in Christ (Galatians 5:1). Let them see your example of how to reveal the darker side of life while teaching them how to appropriate the grace of God into those areas of struggle.

6. Value Intentionality

It will be easy to lose purpose with your friends, which makes being intentional essential. The gospel-centered life comes with a cross. The temptation to be less real and more shallow speaks to the essentialness of keeping your eye on the goal (Hebrews 12:2).

Jesus never lost sight of His goal. There was joy set before Him, which provided the motivation necessary to endure the process of redeeming hurting, lost, and enslaved people (Hebrews 2:14–15; Matthew 26:38–39). Intentional community building invariably leads to conflict, which is the number one reason people default to superficial community life. It is too hard, and we can be too stubborn.

7. Create Contexts

Because of the challenge of getting people to open up and the time involved in building trust with them, it would be wise to have several contexts where you are connecting with your community. Let them experience you in different settings, doing different things. Traditionally, we have used six different settings in which we sought to do life with our friends.

1. Corporate Meeting – Lucia and I typically touch base with our friends each Sunday morning at our church meeting. These are mostly fun and light

conversation times, though praying and more serious discussions happen, too.

2. Community Life – We do life together in a smaller group setting throughout the year. This context is your small group meeting.

3. Couple's Meetings – We try to have each couple over to our home at least once a month. These meetings have proven to be excellent contexts to build with them more privately. These meetings enhance our group meetings. Historically, we have blocked out each Thursday evening of the month for these times of fellowship.

4. Men – I meet with the men in our small community once a month to talk even more personally about life and God.

Relational Contexts

Corporate Meetings

Small Group Life

Couple's Meetings

Person to Person

Events

Social Media

Doing Life Together

5. Events – We do all kinds of fun things together.

6. Social Media – We are regularly communicating with each other through different types of social media.

Tying It Together

There are five means the Lord provides to help you change. These "means" are not in any particular order, and they are not equally applied. It depends on the person, the time, and the need of the moment as to what "means" is most helpful in a person's life. Here are those "means" of grace:

1. The Lord – God will change you.
2. The Bible – The Word of God will change you.
3. You – There is a requirement for you to change yourself.
4. Situations – The Lord will use situations to change you (Genesis 50:20).
5. People – There is a call to the body of Christ to serve the body of Christ in the change process.

This last point is what can make community life an incredible means of grace, especially if the group comes together with a desire to mature in their sanctification.

Call to Action

The first set of questions is for you to examine your heart regarding biblical fellowship (koinonia). My appeal is for you to spend time with the Lord, discussing what you think about living in community with other believers. It would be helpful to share your thoughts with someone who is close to you. I also recommend you have a solid understanding of the previous two chapters on communication to help you get a better handle on true community.

1. What are the risks of not having biblical fellowship?
2. How close should someone get to you?
3. How honest should you be with others?
4. How close should you pursue the opposite sex in biblical fellowship?

5. What does koinonia look like practically at work, home, roommates, dating, marriage, and non-Christian environments?

6. Can you fellowship at the same level as married people if you are a single individual?

7. Can you have fellowship the same way with all Christians, including your Christian relatives?

8. What hinders biblical fellowship for you?

This second set of questions are the ones Lucia and I regularly ask each other. They always get the ball rolling conversationally as we transparently share our experience with God—the good and the bad of it—with each other.

1. What is the Lord doing in your life?

2. What has the Lord taught you lately?

3. How have you applied what He taught you to your life?

4. Will you help me in this "specific" area of temptation in my life?

5. What have you read or heard that is helping you in your sanctification?

6. How is the grace of God working in a particular area of sin?

7. What specific areas are you struggling?

8. How can I serve you in a particular area of your sanctification?

9. What are some ways in which you are leading your friends?

10. How are you applying the sermon from this past Sunday?

Chapter 26

Reason to Marry or Reconcile

Biff and Mable are in love. When they came to their first premarital counseling session, I asked them why they wanted to get married. Mable explained how Biff finished her thoughts. I privately wondered how she would feel five years into the marriage after he stopped talking.

Then she said he made her feel special. I wondered how she would feel after he became preoccupied with other things like his job. She added that he was handsome and how she could not believe someone as attractive as Biff wanted to marry her. I wondered how she would feel after old age crept up on both of them.

When it was Biff's turn, he said he liked the idea of companionship because he did not enjoy being alone. I wondered how he would feel after she started nagging him about his habits. He said, somewhat sheepishly, that he could not wait to have sex. Both of them had kept themselves pure, waiting for their special day. I wondered how he would feel after the babies came and Mable would be too tired and overwhelmed for romance.

Biff's and Mable's reasons for marriage were not bad ones. I am sure most of us had similar thoughts when it was our time to tie the knot. They were serious about the Lord, and they desired to honor Him in everything. It was easy for me to relate to Biff's desire for companionship. God said it was not good for the man to be alone, and I do not like loneliness either. God created us for community life (Genesis 2:18).

The Father, Son, and Spirit—the first community—made us in their image. It seems common sense would motivate the Lord to create humans to be like them. So, He gave Adam a woman. Good for Biff to desire a wife for himself.

I was also glad Biff was willing to state the obvious: he wanted to get married to be intimate with Mable. There is no reason for him to pretend his sexual drive was not real. It is a healthy desire for people who are called to marry. I respected his honesty. I also liked Mable's desire for a complementarian relationship: she wanted someone to complete her, to finish her sentences. The Lord made Eve to complete her husband and vice-versa.

Not the Best

Though their desires for each other were not wrong, there were a few things about them that caused concern. While they had good reasons for marriage, their reasons were not the best reasons. I hoped to help them see this. Here are three things I shared.

1. All of their reasons were secondary reasons for marriage.
2. All of them were preferences. They were desires, not needs.
3. All of them would more than likely change at some point in their marriage.

Marriage is a permanent, lifetime, unbreakable relationship. The only thing that should break the marriage bond is death. That is why it is important for your primary reason for marriage to be the best reason. Having a secondary purpose as the primary reason for marriage could be the death knell to the marriage.

The strength of any marriage is tied directly to the reason for the marriage. If the reason goes away, the strength of the marriage is weakened. That is why I privately wondered what would happen when Biff stops talking, does not make Mable feel special, or becomes less handsome. What if Mable begins to nag him or if she wants sex less?

Their reasons for marriage must be stronger than the ones they gave. If not, they will be heading into rough waters without a sound understanding of marriage. They would become the majority report by joining that ever-growing number of unsatisfied married couples.

Strong, maturing, and joy-filled marriages are becoming rare in our Christian culture. No marriage is immune from trouble. In most of the marriage counseling that I have done, there were two common themes.

1. They came to counseling within the first five years of their marriage.
2. They came to counseling after fifteen or more years of marriage.

I rarely counsel couples between the five- and fifteen-year mark. The reason most of my marriage counseling falls within those two groups is that the first five years are typically before the children come, or they are just on the cusp of parenting.

From the fifteen-year mark (and forward), the marriage embarks on the emptying nest period, when the children become more independent (self-reliant) as they prepare to move out of the home. If the young married couple does not access the help they need or make the appropriate adjustments to their marriage before the children come, two things will probably happen.

1. He will be tempted to escape the marriage through his job.
2. She will be tempted to escape the marriage through her children.

They will become two dissatisfied, discontented, and disconnected people who decided to reorient their marriage around their preferred distractions. Though this would not give them a God-centered marriage, they could survive the marriage with their distractions—at least until the kids leave home. At that point, it leaves the couple with nothing to distract them from themselves.

It is not unusual to hear about a couple getting a divorce after twenty-five or thirty years of marriage. Some people are shocked by this news. I am not. They ignored their problems and each other for as long as they could.

After two decades of muddling along, there were no more distractions to keep them together, and the things they never corrected in the early years came

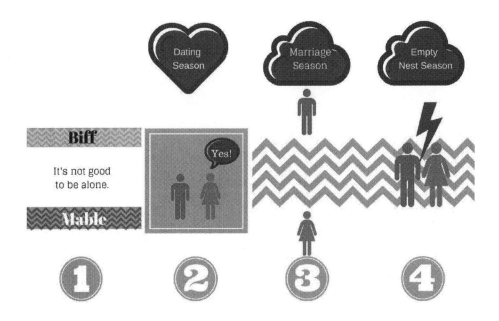

back in force in the later years. The disappointments that passed under the bridge seemed nonreconcilable. They decide to part ways.

The Best

It is imperative that every young couple knows how and determines to build their marriage on the right foundation. It is nonnegotiable for a marriage that not only wants to go the distance but to go the distance with joy.

Before I married Lucia, we began hammering out a Marriage Mission Statement. We were aware of the statistics that pointed toward easy divorce. Nobody needs a good reason for divorce. If you do not like the person you married, all you need to do is play the irreconcilable differences card, and you can get a divorce without much effort.

We were also aware of the number of marriages around us that were not happy. I am not talking about non-Christian marriages but the Christian ones.

We knew many couples who were not exhibiting the love of Christ toward each other. We purposed not to get a divorce or resign ourselves to something less than God's best. That meant we had to build our marriage on something better than what we liked about each other.

- Companionship is great.
- Sex is fantastic.
- Finishing each other's thoughts is a perk.
- Being attractive is a plus, too.

None of those things should receive top billing in any marriage. We needed a better idea. This need is why we began to think about the implications of the gospel as it related to our marriage. We began to view our future marriage through a gospel lens.

Why Marry?

We went after the "why to marry" question by thinking about Christ—the gospel. Why did He come? Redemption. Christ came to redeem fallen man to Himself. We concluded there had to be a redemptive element to our marriage. In Ephesians 5:25–28 Paul gave all marriage partners a picture of the Lord's work by appealing to us to model the gospel in our covenant union. Marriage should be a redemptive image.

"Husbands, love your wives, as Christ loved the church and gave himself up for her, that he might sanctify her, having cleansed her by the washing of water with the word, so that he might present the church to himself in splendor, without spot or wrinkle or any such thing, that she might be holy and without blemish. In the same way, husbands should love their wives as their own bodies. He who loves his wife loves himself" (Ephesians 5:25–28).

Lucia and I began to think about our marriage as a picture of the gospel. We concluded that we could best glorify God by marrying each other so we could project, amplify, or magnify the picture of Christ and the Church more clearly to ourselves and others. We were not thinking about getting married just to be married. Thus, we wrote the following Marriage Mission Statement:

We want to become one flesh because it would allow us to reflect Christ more effectively than by being single. Therefore, we pray our marriage will:

- *Manifest the relationship of Christ and His Church to God.*
- *Manifest the relationship of Christ and His Church to each other.*
- *Manifest the relationship of Christ and His Church to our families and friends.*
- *Manifest the relationship of Christ and His Church to the world.*

We pray our relationship will be a sweet offering to God, a blessing to each other, a testimony to our families and friends, and an opportunity to model Christianity to a world without hope.

As you can see from our Marriage Mission Statement, we clearly crafted a plan to put the beauty of Christ and His Church on display. According to Paul, I am a picture of Christ, and Lucia is a picture of the Church. We both have the high privilege and joyful opportunity to make God's name great through our identification with Him.

It Went Wrong

We became one flesh and quickly did what I privately wondered about Biff and Mable. Even with an excellent plan, our marriage began to crumble. We drifted apart. We failed many times while trying to portray the gospel in our marriage. It was more than just me being a jerk, my hair falling out, or my belly protruding farther than it used to. We slowly changed from the people we were when we had married.

There were three miscarriages. There were job losses. We gained new friends. We lost friends. We changed churches and changed homes. We had lots of money. We had no money. I cannot begin to count how many times I sinned against my wife. It would be safe to say I sinned against her more than I have sinned against any other person in the world.

We have had many desires throughout our marriage. She has had some for me. I have had some for her. We have had some for our life together. Some of them came to fruition, while others fell flat. Through it all, and even in our darkest hours, there has been one constant: our main reason for getting married never changed. In all of our imperfections, we did want to reflect the gospel in our marriage. We work hard at this.

Our world is dying, and we have an incredible opportunity to show them something that cannot be obtained but by Christ alone. Our true heart's desire is not to obscure the picture of Jesus and His Church.

Why Reconcile?

Let me speak ever-so-briefly to the second part of this chapter title: the best reason to reconcile. Perhaps your Marriage Mission Statement is focused on changeable things rather than the unchangeable gospel. Maybe you are not living with the person you married. The things you liked about your spouse seem lost forever. Your spouse has evolved into another kind of person.

Maybe you need to reconcile with your marriage partner. Perhaps you are married, but you are muddling along. Maybe you have a low-grade disappointment as you reflect on how things were versus how things are.

May I appeal to you to begin talking about a marriage redo? May I appeal to you to get some help? You do not have to get a divorce. You do not have to continue down the same old grinding path. You can redefine your marriage, even if you are several years down that road. God is cool with a redo. You can start over no matter how far along you are.

Will you do this? Will you seek help? As you are waiting for help, you can begin to think about what you want your marriage to be. Let the gospel be what defines your marriage. You and your spouse are a picture of Christ and His Church. Begin talking about how to present that picture,

1. As an offering to the Lord,
2. A blessing to each other,
3. A testimony to family and friends, and
4. An opportunity for the world to find hope through Christ.

The first step in this journey back to the gospel will be some long and challenging conversations, but starting is the only way it will work. With your mind fixed on the gospel, which is the process and the goal, begin praying about how to start talking to each other. Invite others into those discussions.

Call to Action

1. If you are thinking about marriage, take the content of this chapter and start writing out your Marriage Mission Statement.
2. If you are married but need to make some changes in your marriage, I appeal to you to begin doing the same thing. Ask the Father to give you a glorious redo.

Chapter 27

How to Kill Your Marriage

If your marriage is bad, you more than likely are doing some of the following things. These are some of the most oft-repeated mistakes I have seen in poor marriages. They are in no particular order. And if any of these ten bad practices characterize your marriage, I have ten tips at the end that can help you have a wonderful marriage. I've also added some helpful diagnostic questions to help you and your spouse.

These tips are written with a sarcastic tone to highlight the absurdity of implementing any of them into your marriage. A husband read this chapter in tears, as he told me later. He said that he had committed all of them in his marriage. He is divorced today.

___

Tip #1 – Always Have the Last Word

I know James talked about being quick to listen and slow to speak, but if you want to win, you must have the last word (James 1:19). One of the most effective ways to accomplish this is to not listen to your spouse.

What you do while she is talking is formulate what you want to say next. You let her wax on while you're figuring out how to overpower her droning. If she likes to talk a lot and if you're a little slow on the uptake, you will have more time to come back at her.

___

Tip #2 – Get Her with a Cheap Shot

Corrupting speech, like criticism and sarcasm, is effective here. This is counter to Paul's appeal in Ephesians 4:29 about building up the other person, but we're talking about winning. Don't let humility or gospel-centered posturing get in the way here.

Sarcasm literally means to cut the flesh. It's like a meat cutter who cuts away nonvalued parts. When you use sarcasm on your spouse, it's a way to devalue her. No doubt this will put her in her place as you get a leg up on the marriage competition.

Tip #3 – Twist Her Words to Tie Her Up

This tip is for the more advanced pugilist. It requires a certain amount of mental dexterity to twist up your wife, but if she is truly the weaker vessel and if you're any kind of man, you should be able to win this battle, too.

One of the keys here is to harden your conscience (Hebrews 3:7). Perchance the Spirit of God tries to illuminate your mind, you can go into rationalization or excuse mode. This process will efficiently mute your inner voice (Romans 2:14–15). A little self-deception goes a long way.

Tip #4 – Push the "It's Not My Job" Worldview

A man's work is outside the home, and the woman's work is inside the home. Make this Scripture-twisting agenda your own by being the comatose husband: grab the remote and surf the 900+ channels or bury yourself on the Internet.

You can also guilt-trip her by making a few well-placed criticisms about how she keeps the home. The home is your castle, and she's the keeper of it. Most women want to please their husbands, so if you keep the carrot dangled in front of her, she will always be trying hard to please you.

Tip #5 – Never Be Wrong

Admitting your mistakes is a weakness. Though John wants you to confess your sins (1 John 1:7–10), the strong man never has sins to confess. This will require more self-deception on your part, but if you have any game at all, you can pull this off (Hebrews 4:7).

Justification is your best friend. To justify is to declare yourself not guilty. Now, you know only the Lord can justify you, but we're talking about winning, right? If you continually declare yourself not guilty, your wife will soon get the message and give up trying to convince you of anything. You will win, and she will be sufficiently defeated.

Tip #6 – Withhold Encouragement

Paul talked about how kindness is the ingredient the Lord uses to motivate a person to change (Romans 2:4). To be kind is to build up. It's a way to motivate by grace. Always looking for evidence of God's kindness in your husband's life is what I'm talking about. Don't do that.

If you withhold encouragement, he will become demoralized. This result is what I call the "whupped pup syndrome." If you're not kind to him, he will begin to shut down. Your once strong and confident guy will fold like cheap laundry.

Tip #7 – Nag Him to Death

The last tip was about withholding something. This tip is about giving him something. Become the dripping faucet Solomon talked about in Proverbs 27:15. Your critical words will be like little sharp daggers in his heart.

Eventually, he will die by a thousand paper cuts. To withhold encouragement while being critical of him is the perfect one-two punch that will end in a knockout every time. You will quickly have him waving the white flag, if not seeking encouragement from someone else.

Tip #8 – Be Oversensitive

The key for this tip is to put him on eggshells. This is a counter-intuitive move: the way to win is to be weak. It's kind of like the Bible (2 Corinthians 4:7). Kind of. But if you pervert the fragile vase Peter talked about (1 Peter 3:7), by being emotional and irrational, he may acquiesce and give up on the marriage.

You will have him so paranoid that he'll be afraid to say or do anything. Keep him guessing. This is your rope-a-dope move. He'll never know how you will respond. At that point, you will own him.

Tip #9 – Overcommit So You're Always Tired

Over-scheduling your life will kill any marriage. Your goal is to always be on the go. Be busy during the day and tired at night. This will motivate him to find other things to do. Just pray the "other things" are not other women, in real life or cyberspace.

If you have children, this will be easy for you. Get them signed up into as many extracurricular activities as possible. Kill marriage time and crank up the van. Worship the sports gods. The key here is to be busy and tired.

Tip #10 – Bring Up Past Wrongs

Never, ever, let go of the past. You will not have to worry about his current screw-ups if you keep prancing the past in front of him. If you and your husband had sex before marriage, it's a done deal. He will never be able to overcome that mistake.

God has wired him to be a leader. The more you remind him of his personal failures, the more you will be able to cut out what the Lord has put into him. Eventually, he will lose heart and accept your assessment: he is a loser.

A Final Thought on Losing

Jesus was a loser according to many people. Even His closest friends were tripped up by His leadership style (Mark 8:32). It got so bad that at the end of His life, they all left Him (Matthew 26:56). They could not accept losing as the way to winning. After all His teaching, they still did not understand the backwardness of the gospel (1 Corinthians 1:18–25).

"But many who are first will be last, and the last first" (Matthew 19:30).

"So the last will be first, and the first last" (Matthew 20:16).

They did not want to be last, and they did not want to lose. They were like us: winning was all that mattered, even if someone had to cut off a person's ear (John 18:10). To actually grab a towel and basin of water was beneath them (John 13:1–17). To give their lives in exchange for someone else was a bridge too far for their selfish minds to grasp (John 15:13; Mark 10:45; Ephesians 5:25). They were myopic in their vision of God's plan for others (Hebrews 12:2).

An ironic twist: if you can't embrace losing, as in being second in your marriage, you will be the biggest loser of all (Ephesians 5:21). Not only will you go down swinging, but you will take your marriage down with you. To win at all costs creates an unbiblical competition between two people. This competition can be most acute within the covenant marriage. When a couple becomes competitors, the marriage is lost. When winning or losing are the most important things in that relationship, the marriage is fast-tracking toward dysfunction.

You will not win at marriage or any other relationship if you refuse to humble yourself by taking on the counterintuitive life of Jesus. This is why I'm leaving you with ten positive tips, plus a few assessment questions to discuss with your spouse. If you can't discuss these things without getting into an argument, please find help now.

Tip #1 – Seek to Listen, Not to Speak

1. How actively do you listen?
2. Is your goal to help your spouse be clear or get your points made?
3. Do you know how to draw out your spouse so he or she can be a more effective communicator?

Tip #2 – Uplift with Your Words

1. Would your spouse characterize you as an encourager? Why or why not?
2. Do you actively seek to find ways to say "thank you" to your spouse?
3. Are you regularly thanking God for your spouse? If not, why not?

Tip #3 – Give Her Space and Grace to Speak

1. Do you create contexts of grace that frees your spouse to express all her thoughts?
2. Do you give your spouse room to make communication mistakes because it's not about saying it perfectly? It's about understanding each other.
3. Are you regularly thinking about your spouse, seeking to understand her more effectively? What does that look like in your marriage?

Tip #4 – Your Job Continues after You Arrive Home

1. Do you proactively plan time with your spouse?

2. Are you regularly asking your spouse how you can be a more effective servant?

3. How do you need to change in these areas?

Tip #5 – You Are Not Entirely Sanctified

1. Do you have a biblical self-suspicion about yourself?

2. Are you quicker to admit your wrongs than your spouse's wrongs?

3. What is it about you that makes it hard to confess your sins to your spouse?

Tip #6 – The Kindness of God Leads to Change

1. Is it impossible for you to keep from saying kind things to your spouse?

2. What does your spouse receive the most from you: your displeasure or your encouragement?

3. What needs to change regarding your communication?

Tip #7 – Contentment Is a Beautiful Jewel

1. How does your spouse experience your discontentment? How do you need to change?

2. Do you regularly identify your grumbling and biblically repent of it? If not, why not?

3. In what ways has your spouse become an idol?

Tip #8 – God Is Your Strength

1. How does the grace of God help you take every thought captive? (See 2 Corinthians 10:3–6.)

2. In what ways are you oversensitive and how does that speak to the idols of your heart?

3. What do you fear regarding your marriage or what are you afraid of in your marriage?

Tip #9 – Calendar Planning Is a Stewardship Issue

1. How do you need to change your calendar to change your marriage?

2. Does your spouse get your best time or your leftover time?

3. How do you both need to change to make each other a "calendar time" priority?

Tip #10 – The Gospel Neutralizes All Sin

1. Are there past sins you and your spouse have not resolved? If not, why not?

2. If past sins are neutralized by the gospel and delivered to God, do you still bring them up for marital review in a punitive way? Why?

3. How does your self-righteousness play out in your marriage? Self-righteousness is a "greater than/better than" attitude.

Will you please talk to your spouse about these things? If that is not possible, will you appeal to your local church leaders to speak into your marriage?

Chapter 28

What Is Your Wife Thinking?

- Boy meets girl.
- They start liking each other.
- They soon figure out ways to spend time together.
- When they are not spending time together, they are strategizing on how to spend time together.
- They become an item.
- A thing.

They are feeling that destiny is in play. If the lovebirds are Christians, their thoughts are about sovereignty and providence: God is in this! It takes little effort to convince them how the good Lord meant them for each other. If they date for a year or less, there will probably be no major disagreements. If they date for a year or more, there will be a few disagreements, but they will persevere through the rough spots.

Any thoughts of not getting married quickly evaporate. God forbid. A bird in the hand is better than whatever may be in the bushes. To start looking for another mate is harder than making a go with the one they have.

They marry.

From the time they meet until their wedding day, they have become closer and closer. Incremental one flesh advancement. Each day revealed more about the other person, and what they learned about each other made them mutually irresistible. This kind of bliss is how things ought to be. A one flesh relationship is a never-ending journey. One flesh-ness is a process of ever-increasing awareness and acceptance until death severs the love bond.

Dating is what makes dating so exciting. It's the beginning of a unique relational adventure. Marriage enhances the journey as more of the mystery about the other person is made clear.

Marriage is like walking into a garden maze, full of beautiful flowers. Each turn reveals another aspect of the other person. The hidden becomes the exposed. Even disappointment does not last because repentance gives them another day that leads to more adventure and enchantment. Paul elevated this kind of Christ imagery in Ephesians 5:25–33, where he talked about the husband being a picture of Christ and the wife being a picture of His church. It is a high call with a great reward for any man or woman who wants to marry.

Ever-Increasing Distance

Then there is sin. Even in the best marriage stories, there is a darker side. The progression toward each other that they began during the dating season hits a few craggy rocks. Disappointment and discouragement begin to capture their optimistic hearts. For various reasons, the pursuit of symbiotic integration starts to lose speed. Instead of two people set on a course to engage and enjoy each other, they readjust, choosing to coexist rather than assimilate. It's the dual silo-effect: twin towers standing side-by-side but never intersecting in a meaningful way.

They become roommates. Business partners. They coexist in parallel. Earlier in their relationship, they could hardly wait to find out about each other. They talked freely and listened attentively. Now the talking is selective, and the listening happens when it is convenient.

They are mostly silent partners. Their communication is no longer an adventure. It is arduous. They learn more about what is going on with each other when they are with their friends. The husband listens as his wife shares her life with her girlfriend. He vicariously "catches up" on the latest happenings because he knows once they return home, the "catching up" on her day slows down, while the frustration that is between them continues to burn.

1. How did this happen?
2. How could two people, who could not keep their hands off each other, grow to a place where they have a lukewarm business relationship?

Weak Gospel

It is unfortunate that few people go into a relationship with the gospel as the animating center of the lives. Without the gospel, no relationship can thrive or mature. People may coexist, but they will not grow in relational warmth. The force of the gospel is the working tandem of reconciliation and transformation. These things get lost in a deteriorating marriage.

Christ came to die so we could be with Him forever. He entered our world and became like us. He lived a perfect life and gave Himself as a sacrifice for us. The Father accepted the work of the Son, which opened the door for reconciliation to and transformation by Him.

As Christ followers, we can live out an echo of the gospel as we engage our relationships. We cannot die for people to save them, but we can die to ourselves with the hope that a selfless sacrifice can be used by God to help others change. There is no relationship where it is more important to model this kind of gospel activity than in a marriage. Paul was not squeamish about this, nor did he hold back on how he thought about a man's responsibility in the marriage.

Paul planted a man's marriage responsibilities right in the heart of the gospel (Ephesians 5:25). Christlike is how husbands are supposed to behave toward their wives. There is no wiggle room here. The gospel is more than a calling. It is an explanation—a definition of how you are to engage your wife.

If a man marries a woman and does not have the gospel as the defining dynamic of his marriage, it will not be long before he spins out of his covenant, ready to give up on his promise. He may stay in the marriage, but his pursuit of his wife will diminish as the years drag on to some inevitable disappointing end. The vibrant life that was in the marriage will die, and the only thing that will sustain their union will be their mutual and agreed upon responsibilities.

No Sin Plan

Without the gospel as the redemptive agent within a marriage, there will be no possibility to fend off the encroachments of sin. We have a gospel because there is sin. Without sin, there would be no need for the gospel.

The conclusion is inevitable: a weakened gospel allows sin to breach the banks of marriage until the couple succumbs to its manipulations. The first sign of sin's advancement will happen within the first year of marriage. As a dating couple, they could not get enough of each other. As a married couple, they are learning the rest of the story—the sinful side of their lives. The things they could hide or keep discreet while dating become front and center in the marriage.

With a weakened gospel and no biblical plan to respond to the problems in their marriage, the partners become sitting ducks. Every sin, whether small or large, slows their one flesh momentum toward each other until they finally decide it's easier to coexist than to work through what is wrong.

This "fake it until you make it" worldview is what begins to shape their thoughts about marriage. It becomes the new standard. Silence sets in and takes over their lives. At first, it becomes small pockets of silence that are between them. With the angry couple left to themselves, these little pockets react like cancer does to the body.

When the cancerous sin entered their marriage, they did not know how to take care of it. Like a stain on a carpet, they left it alone. After a while, there were more stains. They never perceived how such a small thing could metastasize into such a disease.

A Common Scenario

The most common scenario in which this happens is an angry husband. Few things will cause a wife to shut up and shut down like an angry man. The angry man is especially bad if the new wife has not seen this side of her new husband. Even if she has seen it before, there is a monumental difference between dating an angry, harsh, and unkind man and marrying one.

This scenario was Mable's surprise after she married Biff. Within the first six months of their marriage, Biff caught her off guard several times. Mable was a quick study. She learned when she should and should not approach Biff. She learned to be silent.

She learned not to speak her whole mind. Her quietness was when cancer in their marriage was activated. She used to be 100 percent involved in their mutual communication. After the first six months of marriage, she recoiled to about ninety-eight percent. Biff never discerned this because the incrementalization of silence was imperceptible. He was shocked beyond belief when she left him after thirty-two years of marriage. Only then did she give him her full mind. Mable was finally free to be Mable.

After she had done her tour of duty with the children, she believed she deserved a break from her controlling and angry husband. Though she was not justified to leave him, she did it anyway. It was finished.

Do You Know What Your Wife Is Thinking?

Even Christian husbands are notorious for shutting down their wives, while never perceiving they are doing it. They can be too dense, too stubborn, and too righteous to see or admit the adverse effect they have on their wives. It takes a lot of grace and humility for a man to take the lead by owning his role in the deterioration of his marriage.

I have had wives come to counseling for the primary purpose of saying to their husbands what they were afraid to say to them at home. I have had scores of men tell me things they did not know about their wives until it was too late. She left, and after she was away from him, she began saying things she held in for years.

There is a cure for this?

If this is your marriage, I appeal to you. It will take more humility and courage than you have probably ever needed to change the course of your marriage. If you are willing to ask the Father for this kind of grace, you could begin laying the groundwork that could release your wife to be honest and transparent with you.

It may take months for your wife to gain the courage to trust you, especially if you have used anger as a way to keep her shut down and controlled. Even if you offer genuine repentance, she probably will not come out from hiding until she knows it is safe to do so, as evidenced by your practical and measurable transformation.

If you are seeking this kind of corrective care in your marriage, you will need help. The hurts are too deep, and the memories are too fresh. You cannot know what you cannot know, and another set of eyes could serve you well. In addition to finding qualified help, it is essential for you to create an environment of grace for your wife to speak freely. When Lucia and I began making this kind of course correction in our marriage, I asked her if she would do this one thing:

Honey, if you knew you could say anything in the world to me and I would not respond in anger or defensiveness or in any other way that would shut you down, what would you like to say to me?

Of course, this had to be proven. Over a period of months, Lucia began to be more honest with me. She was initially timid because I had tempted her to fear. As she began trusting God and as I appropriated His grace into my life, she began to share things that she would only share with the Lord.

In time, we renewed the adventure we began the first time we met. We chose to fall in love again. Rather than choosing the parallel paths of consenting roommates, we changed our marriage path. We were back on course, incrementally assimilating into each other.

Call the Action

1. Do you know what your wife is thinking?

2. Are there pockets of silence in your relationship?

3. Wife, are you motivating your husband to be open? Are you creating a context of grace for him to be free to speak with you?

4. How vulnerable and transparent are you with each other?

You'll know where you are in your marriage by the freedom or the lack you have in discussing the content in this chapter. If you cannot freely and lovingly talk about what is in this chapter, while assessing each other, your marriage is in trouble.

If you are willing to work on a course correction, I appeal to you to reach out to your church's leadership. Let them inside your marriage. Do not put off getting help today.

Chapter 29

Secondary Considerations

If everything in your life cannot be the most important thing in your life, what is the most important aspect to you? If you were to choose your top priority, aim, or goal in life, what would you choose? What if we begin with a few things that should not be the most important things in your life.

- The sanctification of your spouse is a secondary goal.

- Your children should not be the center of your life.

- Even your children's salvation is a secondary matter.

What would you say is the most important thing in your life and family?

It is imperative that you are clear on the most important thing in your life because that thing will be the grid through which you will do life with God and others. Let me illustrate my point with two fictional case studies. The first one is a husband who has made the sanctification of his wife his chief aim in life. The second one is a dad who has made the salvation of his son his main aim.

My Wife Is My Chief Aim

Jerry's wife, Cyndi, is what some have labeled a shopaholic. She loves to shop, and she loves to spend money. She can no longer walk into her walk-in closet. From floor to ceiling and front to back, the closet is packed with the bounty of her shopping adventures.

Jerry is frustrated. He has cut up her credit cards, took away the checkbook, and put her on an allowance. Last week she took the grocery money and bought a new pair of shoes. On the way to the Sunday church meeting, Jerry noticed her shoes and questioned her about them. She lied. He later found the receipt, which was two days old. Jerry gave her a piece of his mind, which went on for three days. (It was a big piece of his mind, which was not good for either of them.)

- Cyndi has a problem. Cyndi needs help.
- Jerry has a problem. Jerry needs help.

For this chapter, I want to interact with Jerry's problem since it's not as evident. But first, my second illustration.

My Son Is My Chief Aim

Cal is a preacher in a small rural town. He has three children. Two of them have made professions of faith. The oldest son, Tommy, has not made a profession. He's sixteen years old. There are signs that Tommy is not embracing his daddy's religion.

Last week, Cal found out Tommy had been smoking weed. Similar to Jerry, he went ballistic. Cal lectured his son about how he needed to be a Christian. He's probably right. Tommy might not be a believer, and if not, he should be born again (John 3:7). There is a degree of rightness to what Jerry and Cal want.

Their desires are not unbiblical. Cyndi needs help for her addictive behavior. She is legitimately, objectively, and measurably caught in sin (Galatians 6:1). Tommy is also rebelling against God, as observed by his weed smoking and other rebellious behaviors. Though he would not be the first Christian to ever smoke weed, it seems like a fair assumption that he might not be a believer.

The problem, at least in this chapter, is that what Jerry and Cal want is not governed by what should be the most important thing in their lives. They have elevated the sanctification and salvation of their family members to a place that may be in opposition to the Lord's blessing.

The Danger of Stopping Sin

The risk in aiming at a secondary goal is that you might attain that goal—or at least an unbiblical (or sub-biblical) version of it while missing the most important goal in your life. This risk does not mean you should avoid secondary goals. God forbid.

But it does mean you should be aware of some of the pitfalls of overfocusing on secondary goals. Cyndi is representative of one of the more popular secondary goals in Scripture. It's the Ephesians 4:22–24 model of putting off a bad behavior while putting on good behavior.

To put off and put on is an excellent idea. It is essential information to know to live well in God's world. However, it can be misinterpreted and misapplied. For example, it will not work for Cyndi to just put off a bad behavior and put on a good one, which is what Jerry is demanding. That approach is too simplistic and behavioristic, as well as incomplete.

If she does stop her bad behavior and begins a better behavior without dealing with the real motives of her heart, she could quickly become something similar to what Jesus talked about in Matthew 23:27, being pretty on the outside but putrid on the inside.

The Pharisees were the classic scriptural examples of people who looked good on the outside but who were corrupt on the inside. It is likely that, if she does not interact with her heart sufficiently, authentic and sustaining change will not happen. Our modern term for this is behavior modification.

Because the change process can be grueling at times, a discipler, as in Jerry's case, may fall prey to the quick-fix mentality. He can instinctively circumvent the sanctification process because he knows what the desired results should be, which could be a temptation to become more pragmatic in his care for his wife.

Just stop it!

Jerry is looking for immediate results more than he is making sure his wife is changed from the inside out. Demanding behavioral modification, regardless of your good intentions, will blow up in your face.

Jerry is so dialed-in on changing his wife's behavior that he is hindering the process of change. Aren't you tempted to err that way? You can see where the self-destructive behaviors of some people's lives can go, so you ratchet up the intensity of your demands on them to change. A quick-fix sounds reasonable on the surface, but without proper care, you will not get what you want, which is long-term, substantive change.

The Danger of Getting Saved

Cal, the preacher, is making a similar mistake. If you put all your energy into leading a son or daughter or friend to Christ, you may become disappointed, especially if that is your primary focus. Over time you could become discouraged and even bitter, critical, or cynical because your chief aim for them did not happen.

It is a natural temptation for a parent to give into the sin of "controlling worry" because their child is rebellious. There is a vital principle here: the thing that matters the most is the thing that will control you the most. For example, if you are a worried parent, you're controlled by the wrong thing.

This begs another type of question, namely, are you saying that caring about souls—whether it's the salvation or the sanctification of them—is not important? No, that is not what I'm saying at all. You should tell people about Jesus until He comes back. There should never be a time when you are not sending the gospel forth. However, if conversion is your primary focus, you can miss the main thing.

There is no question that it would be monumentally sad if our children rejected the God we serve. We pray regularly for our children, that they will repent of their unbelief and become converted by the gospel. Their need for

252

Christ is one of the reasons we have family discussions, attend church meetings, fellowship with other believers, listen to Christian music, and seek ways to serve.

We do these things because we believe they are the right things to do. Lucia and I think our children need gospel exposure in as many ways and contexts as are appropriate for our pace and season of life. With that said, getting our kids born again is not our primary goal in life. If our primary goal was to lead our children to Christ, we could, for example, fall into the pitfall of placing the main accent of our lives on doing religious things.

In Christian homes where there are Christian activities instead of God-centered relational priorities, those actions could be devoid of substance. Those religious activities could easily slip into routine, be behavioristic, and fill-up calendars, all for the sake of saving the children.

Many so-called Christian homes do Christian things. I've counseled hundreds of people who did devotions every day of their young lives—only to grow bitter and wayward after they became adults.

Their parents did the activities of Christians because they hoped to keep their children from messing up their lives. I'm not saying these parents were not Christians. I'm not even saying they were insincere. I'm saying they allowed secondary priorities to become primary priorities.

Homes with priorities that are not in the right order will be weak. They will miss out on forgiveness, repentance from personal sin, confession, humility, serving each other, personal integrity, transparency, and the biblical modeling of Christ. When the main thing is your children's salvation, there is a good chance that they "ask Jesus into their hearts." What else would you expect?

Expectations like this are usually met when the children are young. Similar to Cyndi, whose "change" was unwittingly enforced by her husband, the children become examples of a manipulated behavioral change.

Your Primary Aim in Life

Paul forever solidified what the most important objective for anyone's life should be. His chief aim was more important than getting people saved or helping them in their sanctification. Be warned: if this is not your greatest aim in life, there will be a high chance you will hurt your relationships, especially those you love the most.

"So, whether you eat or drink, or whatever you do, do all to the glory of God" (1 Corinthians 10:31).

Paul's chief aim is an all-inclusive, transcending goal for your life. Nothing surpasses it. Nothing is of greater value. To glorify God is the chief end of all humanity, and there will be a day when it will come to full fruition. When the Lord rolls up the carpet on time, all people in heaven and hell will glorify God throughout eternity.

"Therefore God has highly exalted him and bestowed on him the name that is above every name, so that at the name of Jesus every knee should bow, in heaven and on earth and under the earth, and every tongue confess that Jesus Christ is Lord, to the glory of God the Father" (Philippians 2:9–11).

There are several ways to define the term "glorify God" as your chief aim in life. One way to say this is to "spread the fame of God." You could say to make "His name great in all the earth." It also carries the idea of "giving Him all honor and respect." It's like standing in holy awe of Him for whom He is.

There are gravity and weightiness to God that humbles you while motivating you to live for Him. This kind of goal compels you to give every part of your mind, soul, strength, will, and heart to Him. (See Deuteronomy 6:5; Mark 12:30.)

It's an attitude, when sufficiently ensconced in your mind, that creates a filter that simultaneously guards your heart while directing your thinking. It guards you against being overcome by sin because the glory of God is more profound to you. It directs you in knowing how to export the Lord to others because the glory of God dominates your thinking.

Whether things are coming to you or you are exporting things to others, the glory of God is the filter through which you make all transactions. Living for God's glory releases you from fear and frustration while giving you the right motive to respond to others.

And this is where Jerry and Cal have been failing. The most important thing in their lives is the obedience of their family members. For Jerry, he wants his wife to stop her sinning ways. For Cal, he wants his son to become a Christian.

Both of these desires are good and great, but because those aims have supplanted what should be the chief aim for Jerry and Cal, they are missing the mark. They are shooting themselves in the foot, as they sabotage their relationships. Their good desires have blinded them from the main thing they should be exhibiting to their families.

Jerry should be exporting the fruit of the Spirit (Galatians 5:22-23) to his wife. Rather than being controlled by his wife's behavior, the Spirit should be controlling Jerry. You'll know if you're controlled by a person's behavior by how you respond to them. If the chief end of all humanity managed Jerry, he would be free from her control, while released to bring a better kind of care to her—a Spirit-empowered, Spirit-illuminated, Spirit-enabled care.

Cal should not be pressuring his son to get saved. He's essentially doing what Jerry is doing, forcing righteousness on another human being. Neither one of them understands how repentance is a gift from the Lord, not a thing manipulated by spouses or parents (2 Timothy 2:24-25).

The Will of Your Father

Having the right perspective is what makes Jesus so amazing. He was not controlled by people's actions, even if those people were blood kin (Matthew 12:46–50). He always zeroed in on His primary purpose in life, and He would not deviate from that main goal.

"For I have come down from heaven, not to do my own will but the will of him who sent me" (John 6:38).

You will have to decide if you're going to do the main will of the Father. Paul told you what that is. If you allow any other aim to transcend that objective, you're going to get off track, which will hurt other people. You are to water and plant, but you are never called to give the growth (1 Corinthians 3:6). Be released from the pressure and the deception of expecting or forcing others to change according to your agendas, plans, and timetables.

Because of the grace of God in you, it is possible to glorify God regardless of what your spouse or children do. But be warned: if you make your chief goal in life the sanctification of your spouse or the salvation of your children, you could very well live a frustrated, disappointed, and anxious life.

Call to Action

1. Do you see the importance of God's glory being your chief aim in life? What does that look like for you? Be specific.
2. You're about to get married. What is the chief aim of your boyfriend or your girlfriend? Be specific. How do you know? Have other people, who know him or her well, shared their opinions with you?
3. You are married. What has characterized your marriage and how you and your spouse do life? What is the center of your life? God's fame? Or, something else? How do you know? Do you agree? What would two of your closest friends say about your chief aim in life as a couple?

Chapter 30

Orientation of Your Home

Jay is passionate about Jehovah. Jenny, Jay's wife, is joyfully following Jay. Jeremy, James, and Jacob, the children, are humbly submitting to their parents. Jack and Jill, the dog and cat, are fat, lazy, and happy. They are one big happy family like they ought to be. They have established the orientation of their home as God-centered. Their family is an excellent picture for you to use to evaluate your home.

Start with the Husband

Husband, your agenda is straightforward: to follow hard after God. The Lord should be your passion, your goal, your life. If you love God more than anything else in your life (Matthew 22:37), you are not only pointed in the right direction, but you have positioned yourself to serve your family the most useful way you possibly can (James 4:6).

If you are leaning heavily into God (Philippians 3:13), you will be sustained and equipped by Him. If your wife is a Christian, she will more than likely follow you with joy. A woman would have to be insane not to desire a husband who is passionately in love with God, as evidenced by him practically being Jesus to her.

Part of your job description is to create an environment that compels your wife to follow you. You should be developing this kind of God-centered momentum in your home. If you are biblically "crazy" about God, your attitude, thoughts, and behaviors toward others will be consistently transforming into the person and work of Jesus (the gospel). Even when you fail, your passion for God will motivate you to repent quickly, which will reestablish the God-centered orientation of your home.

Who's on Point?

If your wife is not following you, I suggest before you begin to critique her, you take a fresh and discerning look at yourself. Before you think about whom she is following, give consideration to whom you are following (Matthew 7:3–5). Who is on point in your home? If the Lord is not the point person of your home, you need to change the leadership structure of your home (1 Corinthians 11:1).

After a lot of living and a good bit of failing, one thing I have learned is I cannot be trusted to be in charge of our home. My wife knows this. So do my children. I have put my sin on display in our home many times (1 John 1:7–10). Hiding failures in a family is impossible. It is no secret to my family how I can mess up things.

It's imperative for Lucia to know that I am not the leader of our family. She needs this assurance. She needs to know that someone more capable than me is leading our home. As you evaluate your home, let these two ideas guide your thoughts and discussions: Who leads your family? Who do you and your wife want to lead your family?

God Replacements

As you think about the orientation of your home, who or what would you say is on point? Who or what pulls your family along? What defines your home? Whoever or whatever is on the point of your family is your functional god.

- Your work?
- Your ministry?
- Your activities?
- Your spouse?
- Your children?

These are important questions. Some may ask how a person in ministry could not have God on the point of his family. The answer to this excellent question is one of the sadder commentaries about the Christian community. It is no secret that the fallout rate among pastors is high, partly due to their inability (or unwillingness) to guide their families biblically. It is also true that the rest of us, who lead small groups and Bible studies, fail in leading our families.

Ignoring family failure can be easy. Being ministry-minded more than marriage-minded is commonplace. Some church leaders' ministry is a way of placing an ointment on the failures in the home. There are also many women in horrible marriages who lead Bible studies. Being an example to their followers is not as important as filling a slot in the church.

Their Bible study can become a refuge—their brief moment of sanity in an otherwise disappointing family dynamic. If you are ignoring marriage and family failure while pursuing ministry activity, what keeps you from dealing with your marriage problems?

1. Is it your reputation?
2. Is it your craving for security?
3. Is it your desires for approval?
4. Is it not a priority of your church?
5. Are you afraid?

Anything that replaces the work needed to put Christ on display in your life, marriage, and family is idolatry. God replacements like these can suck the life out of what should be a vibrant, God-centered home. I have known many men in ministry who have undesirable marriages. Christians place these men on pedestals, praising them for their reputations and skills.

Other husbands and dads spend their waking hours chasing the dollar. The American dream has duped them into pursuing a lie. They want the right neighborhood, the right job, the beautiful wife, activity-centered children, and the approval of their circle of friends.

Too often, Christianity becomes a tack-on to their lives. Religion is a means to be connected to the right people while providing morality-based training for their children. Nominalism is a dangerous business. God is not the point and purpose of these families.

The fallout is inestimable.

Clogging the System

Have you ever sat in traffic behind a car that was not moving? All the other cars were moving, but you were in the only stopped line. The person in front of you was texting. That is what a wife feels like when her husband is not passionately pursuing God. He is preoccupied with other things. The Godward momentum of her family gridlocks because her husband is not progressing in his walk with the Lord. When the man is not moving forward, it hinders everyone behind him.

In the movie, My Fair Lady, Eliza Doolittle was at the racetrack pulling for her favorite horse, Dover. Eliza was a lower-class Cockney flower girl who was being trained by Henry Higgins in the ways of a proper lady. She was put to the test when asked to have tea at the track with some of the upper crust.

She did well until the race was closing in on the finish line and her horse, Dover, was not moving fast enough. As the horses were heading toward the line, Eliza, in a momentary lapse into desperation, yelled, "Dover, move your blooming arse!" As you might imagine, all the proper ladies choked on their tea. They were flabbergasted.

Though a Christian woman might not say it exactly the way Eliza did, that is how many of them feel when their husbands are not leading in the sanctification of their home. It is as though the wife is running up her husband's backside because of his lack of spiritual forward movement. If your marriage and family are stagnating like this, here are a few questions for your consideration:

1. Husband, does your wife humbly ask you to follow the Leader of your home?
2. Do you have a hunger for God and a desire to follow Him as your family follows you?
3. Do you know how to lead this way?
4. Are you embarrassed to lead your family because you feel like a hypocrite?
5. Wife, how are you encouraging and motivating your husband to lead you?
6. Do you nag him? Are you critical of your husband?
7. What is he more aware of: your critique and nagging or your encouragement and motivation?
8. Can you and your spouse talk about the leadership failure in your home?

Talking about Leadership Failure

The first step in reorienting your home to God is to be able to speak about what is wrong with it. You will not be able to do this without the humbling power of the gospel working in both of your hearts. If you cannot talk about what has gone wrong in your marriage, you will need a gospel reorientation of the heart so you can have a gospel reorientation in your marriage and family.

Only humble people can talk about what is wrong with them. Couples who cannot honestly and humbly share their faults and failures with each other have drifted far from the truths proclaimed on Golgotha's hill. A man or woman who knows where they came from has nothing to prove, nothing to hide, and nothing to protect (1 Timothy 1:15). The gospelized person is not afraid of what others may know about him because he is resting in this truth:

I was once a lost sinner, but now I am saved. I am the Lord's beloved child; His approval is all I need. By grace, God saved me. I do not fear what others think about me or what they may say about me. God has declared me free, not guilty, and pleasing to Him. The works of Christ define me. (See Romans 3:23; Ephesians 2:8–9; Mark 1:11; Hebrews 11:6, Proverbs 29:25)

1. What hinders you from talking about how each of you has failed the marriage?
2. Husband, can you address your failures without attaching her failures to yours?
3. Will you humbly ask your wife how you can lead her more effectively?
4. Wife, can you address your failures without justifying or defending them?
5. Will you humbly let him know how he can lead you more effectively?

The two most common misapplications regarding the orientation of the home concept are the child-centered home and the passive husband.

Child-Centered – Some families put their children on point. Everything centers around the children. The typical mom in the child-centered home can spend ten to fifteen years of her life in a minivan, caving to the culture's expectations for children, which is to cart them around and keep them activity-centered.

These children become increasingly self-centered, as life revolves around what they want to do. They rarely learn humility, respect, and submission. They are also typically weak when it comes to serving others. They don't know how to serve because it's not their habit (Mark 10:45).

Passive Husband – Another common problem in a family gone wrong is the spiritually passive male. The passive husband home is where the wife takes on more of the spiritual leadership, while the man is preoccupied with other things that feed his self-centered preferences.

The child-centered, passive-husband home is upside down. Typically, the child and the dad are in the same home, since the lazy dad opens the door for the child to be the center of attention. Most parents don't realize the monster they are creating until the child becomes a teenager.

Call to Action

If the orientation of your home focuses on the wrong person or things, please understand there is no way to correct what is wrong unless you both are willing to sit down and talk about it and make a practical plan to change.

If you cannot talk about what's wrong, I appeal to you to find someone who can walk with you through the problems in your home. The wrong orientation of the home rarely auto-corrects. If it continues, the future fallout will break your heart. There is only one right way for the home to function: the Lord must lead, and everyone else must practically follow His leadership.

1. Will you talk about the questions put forth in this chapter?

2. Will you set aside some time to talk about your marriage?

3. If not, will you find someone to help you and your spouse?

4. Are you in a church that values your marriage over your ministry?

5. If only one of you is willing to make changes, will you begin making those changes today?

Chapter 31

Are You a Restful Soul?

Let's free associate: When you think about rest, what goes through your mind? What does rest mean to you and how do you obtain it? Here are a few examples of how some people pursue rest.

1. A husband comes home from a long day at work and crashes in front of the television.

2. A wife hustles from the car line at the school where she just dropped off her kids to rendezvous with a friend at Starbucks.

3. A friend is struggling through life. The disappointments are steady. She finds rest through medication.

4. A teen spends a couple of hours surfing the net—a routine which helps him escape the madness of his world.

5. A family leaves for their planned vacation. A week later they collectively crave another week to recover.

The one thing these attempts to find rest have in common is how the different strategies are cultural, not biblical. Most people perceive rest as being a behavioral escape from life rather than a permanent condition of the soul. Wrong thinking about rest is what makes it so elusive. If you don't know what it is, you will not find it.

The average worker lives for the weekend, as though the primary purpose of the weekend is a time of rest. Rest is not the purpose of weekends. Our culture concocted weekends to get away from work, not as a cure for the rest problem. When the Bible talks about rest, it never speaks about weekends, vacations, evenings out, catching a movie, or any other commonly perceived idea that is supposed to refresh us.

Seeking escapes from stress is different from entering into rest. Let me press the point further. Weekend retreats, Bible conferences, or youth camps are not designed to give you the Bible's version of rest either. Biblical rest is not a singular action in the timeline of life, but rather, it is a gift the Lord gives to you.

Resting in the Storms of Life

"But he was in the stern, asleep on the cushion. And they woke him and said to him, 'Teacher, do you not care that we are perishing?'" (Mark 4:38).

There were several men on a boat in a storm. One of them was sleeping. The rest of the people were frantic, fearful, and faithless. One of them knew the secret to rest. The remainder anticipated a time of rest after they escaped the storm. Are you like the disciples?

Your storm may be your job, marriage, family, church life, peer pressure, economic struggle, persecution of various kinds, as well as other disappointing events and troubling people in your life. You're not on a boat, but you are in a storm. It is possible that you are not at rest but frantic. You are fearful. Sleeping in your storm like Jesus did may be as foreign to you as Jesus dying on a cross to save you.

Is your native thought, like the disciples, to escape your troubles? The temptation to believe rest will come after the storm passes is common. Soul recovery does not happen that way.

"All things are full of weariness; a man cannot utter it; the eye is not satisfied with seeing, nor the ear filled with hearing" (Ecclesiastes 1:8).

A search for rest by changing your venue or circumstance is like chasing a mirage in a desert. It will leave you weary. What you think you see will not satisfy and what you hope to hear will not fulfill. This kind of worldview and practice is carnal and insatiable.

"Remember also your Creator in the days of your youth, before the evil days come and the years draw near of which you will say, 'I have no pleasure in them'" *(Ecclesiastes 12:1).*

As your body continues to waste away (2 Corinthians 4:16), you'll become increasingly hardened, cynical, frustrated, and hopeless. Your quest for the culture's version of rest will not bring pleasure. For those people, God quickly becomes a faint byline in their minds, which leaves them giving up and despairing.

The Lord's Rest Is Different

"Let us therefore strive [work] to enter that rest" *(Hebrews 4:11a).*

Rest is a provision from the Lord, not something found in the world. God is the author and dispenser of it, and, thankfully, He planned for you to enter into His rest. God's priority for your rest is a serious matter that requires your utmost attention because the devil broke the shalom your soul craves, which is why you're tempted to find peace through man-centered methods (Genesis 3:7).

"And the peace of God, which surpasses all understanding, will guard your hearts and your minds in Christ Jesus" *(Philippians 4:7).*

To rest is to be godlike (Genesis 2:2–3). When God rested on the seventh day from His creative acts, the rest was not from exhaustion. The Lord is omnipotent. He was not tired. The rest God took was a rest of satisfaction rather than a break because He was physically whooped. Work and rest are not at odds with each other. The Lord never stops working, and He is always at rest.

The rest He took after He had created the world was a rest of satisfaction, contentment, and pleasure as He reflected upon His acts. He was not taking a break or looking for a day off from work. He was enjoying what had just happened. Creator God found rest (satisfaction) from forming the world. The Son of God experienced satisfaction (rest) during a dark and stormy night. Rest is not dependent on contexts, but it is a condition of the soul.

The Lord's Rest Is Communal

"Let us therefore strive to enter that rest" (Hebrews 4:11a).

When the world thinks about rest, their thoughts almost always go toward self-centered, individualized, relaxation for the pursuit of personal enjoyment. This kind of rest has a "separation from community" component to it. Though there can be some benefit to taking breaks from people, this is not the primary kind of rest the Lord wants for you. The rest of the passage in Hebrews 4:1–11 speaks of a community language: us, them, and they.

The writer is not talking to a person but to a body of individuals. The kind of rest God is calling you to is a communal rest (Hebrews 13:3). He is appealing to "us" to rest. It's not a call for an individual to chill out for a while on an island but to collectively enjoy rest as a right and privilege for the whole body of Christ.

The Lord wants all of His children to enjoy His rest. You are the body of Christ, and you all should be working hard to find this rest. Though you will benefit from the fullness of this rest in heaven, you can enter into it today. God's forever future and perfect rest-filled world has come backward into your present day through the person and work of Jesus. Though it is not entirely here, it is truly here. You can enjoy the eternal reality of rest right now.

The Lord's Rest Is Serious

"He said to them, 'Why are you so afraid? Have you still no faith?' And they were filled with great fear and said to one another, 'Who then is this, that even wind and sea obey him?'" (Mark 4:40–41).

What if the Son of God did not have rest in the storm but was just as frantic and fearful as his friends were on the boat that night? If that were the case, their reaction to Him would have been different.

The rest God gives to you is radically different from what the world expects and seeks. The gospel is a counter-intuitive way of living (1 Corinthians 1:18–25). There is a reason for this: the Lord is glorified as His calming and sustaining power works through you (2 Corinthians 4:7).

If Jesus acted like them, He would not be worth following. Who wants to follow someone who can have their shalom so easily discombobulated? You do not need the rest the world can offer. You need the rest God provides. Not accessing God's rest is what makes a lack of God's rest so dangerous. To not have it or not to enter into it is to make a joke out of the work of Christ. Think about all the work the Lord went to give the children of Israel rest.

To not enter God's rest is like trampling the blood of Jesus under your feet. To stand on the wilderness side of the Jordan River, refusing to obey the Lord by not entering into His rest is high treason. The Hebrew writer called it disobedience: "Let us, therefore, strive to enter that rest, so that no one may fall by the same sort of disobedience." (See Hebrews 4:11.) Finding and enjoying the Lord's rest is a matter of faith and obedience.

How to Work for God's Rest

When the winds and storms come into your life, and you are resting in those challenges, God is exalted, you are satisfied (at rest), and people are amazed. You are not diminishing His work in you but drawing attention to the greatness of your God.

You are making a bold statement about your satisfaction in Him and how it trumps your situational difficulties. Your confidence in God is other-worldly shalom that surpasses human comprehension (Philippians 4:7).

Just as the disciples asked, "Who then is this," your sphere of influence will be just as perplexed and curious about what's up with you (Mark 4:41). Don't you want to give your friends a taste of something that is different from waiting for a dissatisfying weekend?

- How are you striving for God's rest in a world where there is no rest?
- How do you enter into the Lord's rest?

Faith

"And they said to Joshua, 'Truly the LORD has given all the land into our hands. And also, all the inhabitants of the land melt away because of us'" (Joshua 2:24).

Obedience

"Then Joshua rose early in the morning, and they set out from Shittim. And they came to the Jordan, he and all the people of Israel, and lodged there before they passed over" (Joshua 3:1).

Did you see what Joshua and his friends did to enter into God's rest? They believed, and they obeyed. That's it. Unbelief and disobedience mean the Lord has not given "all the land into your hand," and you are not going rise "early in the morning and set out" for God's rest.

"So also faith by itself, if it does not have works, is dead" (James 2:17).

270

You enter into rest by obedience and belief. Obedience is about radical-believing-dependence, which is what it takes to join the rest in the here and now.

1. Do you believe you are more than a conqueror because of Him who died for you (Romans 8:37)?

2. Will you enter into His rest as an act of obedience, as you base your faith in the gospel?

Rest is not about laziness but about working because of God's provision that highly motivates you. You anchor biblical rest in the character and work of God. Real rest in God should excite some activity in you to strive for a greater experience of God.

Taste the Lord

"Oh, taste and see that the LORD is good! Blessed is the man who takes refuge in him!" (Psalm 34:8).

Jesus found refuge (rest) while in the storm. He tasted and saw how the Lord was good. He was a blessed man. The most rest-filled people are those who are relentlessly pursuing God while finding their rest in Him. This requirement brings you to the gospel. Either it is real, or it is not. Either it can do for you what the Bible says in can do, or it cannot. You are called to engage the gospel by practicalizing it into your life.

If you do not have God's rest, you must begin with the gospel. Have you tasted it and found the Lord to be good? Are you affected by the person and work of Christ to where your faith and obedience is animated and evident to all? If not, may I recommend two things?

1. Stop the futile search to find rest in the world. Weekends, materialism, relationships, status, jobs, or any other means to escape from trouble and disappointment will not deliver rest.

2. Strive to taste the true and living God. Find rest in the depths of God. Be warned: you will have to fight, strive, and work to engage, enter, and enjoy God's rest. You will find rest on a cross, not at the beach soaking in the rays.

Chapter 32

Improve Your Prayer Life

Dear Rick,

I have a question regarding the daily practice of prayer, hoping to gain a perspective from others. Ever since God saved me about ten years ago, I have had a deep conviction to pray. When I was a new convert, I asked others how they prayed and read books on the subject.

Unfortunately, a legalistic environment poorly nurtured my ideas about prayer for six years. It became an issue because if I missed my morning prayer time, I was depressed all day because I believed that I had lost God's favor. I would not have said that, but it is the way I lived. I still struggle with it today. Over the last few years, as I have begun to understand the gospel better, I have by God's grace tried to remind myself that grace through faith leads to salvation.

Even in moments when I have not had the opportunity to pray as I ought, I have said something like, "Lord, thank you that I am no less your son though I'm rushing right now, but I can have joy in believing, regardless of my prayer life."

That being said, my deep conviction to pray has never left, and a lot of time I find it hard (though I hate to say it) to fit prayer into my life. At this season of my life, I am extremely busy.

My schedule makes it hard to pray consistently. If I let the day get away from me, it is hard to stop and spend quality time in prayer. Sometimes this routine can drag on, and I feel worse and worse.

1. Do you think I should toughen up, live on less sleep, and get up early?

2. Should I rearrange my work schedule if I can?

3. *Should I learn to turn every distraction off at some point during the day other than the morning and seek God then?*

I understand Jesus saves me. I know He is always with me. My relationship with the Lord is the greatest treasure in my life, and I am willing to change what I have to. I would love some help regarding my prayer life.

Our Common Struggle

Prayer is every Christian's dilemma and tension. Many Christians struggle to have a consistent and dynamic prayer life. It reminds me of athletes who do not stretch before they run. Most runners do not take the time to stretch. Running is the main thing; stretching is a mundane precursor to the main thing.

Engaging your day is the main thing; prayer can feel like a mundane warm-up, but if it is valued, it will make the race a more enjoyable experience. Though you know this, you may struggle to value prayer enough to implement it into the fabric of your daily life.

I have given a lot of thought to your struggle with prayer because I have experienced it ever since the Lord regenerated me in 1984. Your struggle is my struggle. When I think about how to make my prayer life better, these eight things come to mind. I hope they will help you.

1 – Stop Praying – Start Talking

The first thing I recommend you do is to move the word "prayer" to the back of your vocabulary list—at least for now—and replace it with the word "talk" or talking to the Lord. The Lord is a person, not an object. I think sometimes we think about the Lord the way other religions bow to their objects and idols.

Bowing and talking to an object is like talking to a sign post. It is impersonal, unidirectional communication that is not warm or reciprocated. Prayer can connote that kind of attitude for some individuals: God is a distant deity rather than an immanent person, which can make prayer colder than ice and chore-like rather than a lively conversation between two people.

Call to Action – Stop right now and talk to the Lord. Say something to Him. Right now!

---

2 – Be Friends with the Lord

I recommend you use the word friend for how you think about the Lord. You can think about Him in many other ways, which you should, but what if you make the word friend common-speak when you think about Him?

"'Abraham believed God, and it was counted to him as righteousness'—and he was called a friend of God" (James 2:23b).

Jesus wants us to think about Him as a friend (John 15:15). This idea will help to soften the rigidness from your former legalistic presuppositions and worldview—the way you used to view Him. The Lord is both transcendent and imminent. You hold Him in awe, power, majesty, and wonder, and He understands your most painful struggles and frustrating temptations. God is also near you.

Based on what you said about legalism, I imagine it's easier for you to think of Him in a courtroom rather than a living room. You want to reverse this, especially when thinking about prayer.

Call to Action – Do you experience the Lord more in the courtroom or the living room? Why did you answer the way you did?

---

3 – Unlimited Talk Time

You may not be married, but I am going to use a marriage analogy here. I think about the Lord—in the context of this chapter—the way I think about my wife. She is my friend, my best friend in life. I talk to her throughout the day, at different times during the day, and through various means: phone, text, verbal.

I think about her often because she is my friend. I have pictures of her on my desk and in my heart. This kind of ever-present awareness is how I engage the Lord. I do not phone or text Him, of course, but I do engage Him throughout my day with short messages (prayers) or longer talks (prayers). You must make this your habit.

"For his invisible attributes, namely, his eternal power and divine nature, have been clearly perceived, ever since the creation of the world, in the things that have been made. So they are without excuse" (Romans 1:20).

Call to Action – Ask the Lord to change your talk plan to an unlimited plan.

---

4 – Talk about Everything

If you have an unlimited talk plan with the Lord (which you do), don't worry about using up your minutes: talk to Him about everything, at any time, all the time. Isn't this what you do with best friends? If you have an idea, share it with the Lord. You will never talk too much to God. Create that kind of talk habit.

Let Him become your best friend with whom you want to share all your thoughts. That means you are not just asking Him for things, but you are thanking Him for things. Tomorrow, as you go to work, survey your surroundings; thank Him for those things that He brings to your mind.

Talk to Him.

Ask Him questions.

Say "thank you" for what you observe.

Call to Action – After you finish this chapter, thank the Lord for what you read and share with Him a useful tidbit you took from the chapter.

5 – Structure and Spontaneity

There are times when my wife and I cannot find adequate down time to talk. Even so, that does not alter our relationship. Last night we talked from 11:30 p.m. to about 1:30 a.m. We were talking about life, family, friends, and how to do life more effectively with others. It was a great conversation. It was satisfying and spontaneous.

We also have scheduled date times, which are analogous to dedicated times of prayer in a closet. Typically, we will go to a dinner or some other place. It is rarely about the place but about being with each other. We are friends who talk to each other at different times, in different ways, and about different things.

The Lord is your friend, and you need to speak to Him in as many ways as you can create. Some of your time with Him will be structured, dedicated prayer times, but most of your talk times should be spontaneous. If you pray in a structured context for fifteen or twenty minutes, you will have fourteen to eighteen hours for random talking possibilities left to enjoy.

Call to Action – Where is your structured place of prayer? If you do not have one, create one.

6 – Be Free from Legalism

Legalism is the bane of praying. It will choke the life out of your prayers while filling you with doubt and frustration. Praying every day at the same time in the same place is not a bad idea, but it should not be a hill of legalism to die on because it is not possible to do. As much as I love my wife, I cannot maintain that kind of commitment to her.

Prayer is not a competition with yourself to be perfect. Prayer is only part of your relationship with the Lord, and if that relationship morphs to the point of legalistic conditionalism, your relationship will be a struggle.

If you can pray every morning at such a time, by all means, pray at that point, but do not let that time define your relationship with the Lord. If you miss it, do not think the Lord is displeased with you. That is not how a loving relationship is defined.

Call to Action – If you pray and have a good day, did you have a good day because you prayed? What if you did not pray and had a bad day. Did you have a bad day because you did not pray? There are legalistic answers to my questions, and there are gospel-centered ones. What were your answers?

---

7 – Be Dependent

One of the ways I talk to my Friend is when I write. I write as though the Lord is at my elbow. I ask Him about the content I am creating. For example, I asked Him what I should say to you. I thanked Him when I finished for how He shaped my thoughts. That is just one way I can demonstrate my dependence on Him.

Think about how you can create opportunities to show your dependence on Him. Ask Him for help regarding all matters of life, big and small. Some of those times will be structured prayer moments, but most of them will happen in the milieu: the day-to-day contexts in which you live. "In the milieu" praying is what keeping in step with the Spirit means. Each step you take, your best Friend is at your side.

Call to Action – What hinders you from being God-reliant over self-reliant? Whatever that thing is, ask the Lord to take it from you.

8 – Enjoy Variety

There are at least four kinds of prayers: wow, help, thanks, and please. Think through how you can implement all of them into your life.

"Wow, dear Lord, you are amazing." Wow-type praying is when you are perfectly overwhelmed at the bigness, greatness, and all-powerfulness of the Lord. When the finite tries to wrap his brain around the Infinite, all he can do is prostrate himself on the ground in stunned amazement.

"Help me, dear Lord. I need you." This type of praying gets at the heart of your needs. You are in that place again where you need help, and you know the only person who can help is God Almighty, so you ask Him to impose Himself into your life and situation.

"Thanks, Lord. You are so kind to me." Then there are gratitude prayers. This type should be rolling off your tongue every waking hour. There is never enough time in the day to thank the Lord for all you have experienced from Him through your five senses. Gratitude praying should be the most frequent praying you do.

"Please help my friend." One of the greatest honors you can bestow on friends is to take their needs to the King of the universe. This kind of praying is Christlike, as it imitates the One who intercedes for you. Whether it is in structured or spontaneous moments, praying for others is a gracious gift to your friends and a sweet aroma before the Lord.

Call to Action – How are you doing with these four types? How do you need to change?

Chapter 33

Stop Reading - Start Doing

"But be doers of the word, and not hearers only, deceiving yourselves" (James 1:22).

Mandy has been in a Bible study for eleven consecutive years. She loves her Bible study. It is the third Tuesday of each month from 7:00 to 8:30 p.m. Mandy shows up at 7:00 sharp and promptly leaves at the last "amen." Mandy also has a dysfunctional marriage, fifteen years running.

Mark reads his Bible from cover to cover every year. Bible reading has been his passion and conviction for the past nine years. He also rarely misses his morning prayer time. Mark is married to Mandy.

As a couple, they are hitting all the Christian marks. They attend their local church meeting every Sunday, nearly without exception. They are involved in their gender groups. They are consistent in the spiritual disciplines, but their marriage has gone from rocky to rockier.

There is something wrong with their Christian game plan. It is not working. Mark and Mandy are learning but not transforming. They talk at length about their latest study or how thankful they are to be part of a local body that provides so much, but the divide between them continues to grow.

The Best Defense Is a Good Offense

"So whoever knows the right thing to do and fails to do it, for him it is sin" (James 4:17).

After asking a few insightful questions to Mandy, it became apparent that one of the reasons she liked her structured Bible study was because it allowed her to show up, sit down, soak in, and quickly leave as soon as it ended. The structure of the Bible study did not challenge her by asking questions that probed the real condition of her life and marriage. It was mostly a sit and soak session that required little from her. She liked it that way.

Her biggest challenge was navigating the spontaneity of the break time without being engaged about the personal things in her life or marriage. Attending Bible study was her way of being in control while tacitly participating in Christianity but not being exposed or challenged. She had a false intimacy with God and her friends.

Mark accomplished similar things, though he went about it another way. Mandy would be private in a group setting, while Mark did his devotions in a private setting. Their best defense was being on the spiritual-discipline-offensive. They were hiding in plain sight.

Their stellar attendance and consistent disciplines moved them to the head of the class, but their lives were not transforming. Their marriage is inching toward increasing dysfunction, and now that their children are in the early teen years, it is affecting the whole family.

The tenor of the home has the feel of smoldering anger. Everyone "gets along" though everyone knows it's a fake perseverance at best. Mark and Mandy figured out how to coexist in the Christian world while maintaining ongoing displeasure with each other.

This fictional story is not fictional with untold millions of professing Christians. They are involved in all the right Christian things, but Christianity is not intruding their lives in such a way that is transformational.

In most cases like this, no one ever learns the real story, not until something blows up in the marriage or with the children. When this happens, someone calls the Christian medics while the onlookers are scratching their heads, wondering how this could happen to such a stellar couple.

Discipleship Hindrances

"Work out your own salvation with fear and trembling" (Philippians 2:12b).

There could be many reasons for what is wrong with Mark and Mandy. Their story is certainly not an anomaly. I have counseled many couples like this and have discovered a few common denominators. Here are two of them.

No Transparency – The most obvious hindrance is they did not want to be exposed. Being transparent may be one of the hardest things for a Christian to do. Sometimes a lack of transparency is born out of a fear of being hurt or slandered.

Though it is a legitimate fear, it is one that denies the power of the gospel. The fearful person who resists transparency has not appropriately dealt with this question: Is God's opinion of you more controlling than any other person's opinion of you? If God's opinion has more control over you, then you will be less likely to hide, even with the possibility of being hurt by others. That is the power of the gospel working in a person's heart.

Another reason for a lack of transparency is because the person is hiding some sin. Sinful living can only thrive in inhabited darkness. Nobody can serve two masters; one will have dominion over the other (Matthew 6:24). When you couple hidden sin with a fear of being exposed, you can guarantee the person will not come clean or find help. Christian disciplines will not help this kind of person, though it can provide a cover for him to operate.

Discipleship can only happen when a person is willing to be completely honest about his life. This kind of discipleship occurs in the contexts of honesty and transparency. Without these two things, a Christian is not growing but going through the motions.

Ignorance – It is possible that Mark and Mandy do not know how to disciple each other. You may be surprised to know the most common answer I hear when I ask a husband how he disciples his wife is, "I don't know how to do that."

If they give an answer at all, it is usually along the lines of doing devotions, praying together, or going through a book. While those things could supplement any relationship, they should not be the centerpiece of a relationship.

When books, devotions, and prayer time supplant redemptive communication, the community will deteriorate. It is rare for me to counsel a couple who has not read more than one book on marriage.

It is also rare for me to counsel someone who does not have a working knowledge of the Bible. Books, Bibles, and prayer are almost always part of what a couple has tried to rejuvenate their marriage, only to be disappointed because those things did not work. If I were to counsel Mark and Mandy, I would hyperbolically tell them something along these lines:

I want you both to stop reading your Bible, stop reading all those books, stop praying, stop doing your devotions, and start talking to each other. It's radical, I know. You both know enough about the Bible to choke a Pharisee. You do not need more Bible knowledge, and your prayers are being hindered and rendered ineffective by God (1 Peter 3:7) because you are missing out on one of the most common-sense things you can do: talk to each other.

Knowledge Plus Application

"For though by this time you ought to be teachers, you need someone to teach you again the basic principles of the oracles of God. You need milk, not

284

solid food, for everyone who lives on milk is unskilled in the word of righteousness, since he is a child. But solid food is for the mature, for those who have their powers of discernment trained by constant practice to distinguish good from evil" (Hebrews 5:12–14).

Mark and Mandy need to learn how to communicate with each other. They both are unique people, made by God, shaped by sinful means, and in need of someone coming alongside them to unpack them according to how sin has developed them and how God wants them to be.

For example, Mark needs to set aside all his Bible reading and praying and start exegeting another kind of book—his wife. He does not have a knowledge problem; he has an application problem. He could spend the next forty years reading his Bible and praying every day and still end up in divorce court. His Bible reading and prayer life will not help him until he gets in front of his wife and they begin talking honestly and openly.

One of the reasons churches offer so many Bible studies is because it is easier to tell someone what to do through a study than it is to get into the trenches of their lives where the sin is real, feisty, nasty, and complicated. Mark and Mandy need confronting, not more information about what the Bible teaches. They need some friends who can discern their lives and are willing to cut through the nonsense and help them.

Bible studies and prayer vigils will not do this. Those things are essential, but they are passive ways for sanctification to happen. They are part of how to mature in Christ, but if they are the only parts, Mark and Mandy will not grow in Christ. They will become smarter but not more sanctified.

I'm not dissing studying the Bible or praying. I am saying if you know the Word but are not practically engaging your relationships with the Word, you're dishonoring God and hating your relationships. People can spend a lot of time praying and studying while their families spiral in dysfunction.

I make a living counseling biblically educated Christians. There is something wrong with that statement. It should not be that way. Christian transformation is knowledge plus application, not just knowledge alone.

How to Apply

If you are a person who is not maturing in Christ or if you are in a relationship that is not growing in Christ, here are two things for you to consider.

Are You Transparent?

Without making excuses for why you are not transparent, the question is, are you transparent? If you are not, you will not mature in Christ. The gospel has the power to transform you, but it will be impotent in your life if you are not willing to engage it the right way.

Part of the right way is for you to be engaged by the gospel in the context of community. If you are not willing to be transparent in your community or if you do not have a community that can know you the way you need to be known, you will hinder your growth in Christ.

Are You Hiding Something?

Counseling can be a lying profession. People lie to me all the time. I do not personally struggle with this, though I do sometimes wonder why someone would want to meet with me to talk about personal or marital problems and choose to lie.

If you want to change, you must be honest about what is going on in your life. You cannot reveal half the cards in your deck and expect anyone to speak intelligently into what you need to change. Transformation does not work that way.

Call to Action

If you are willing to be fully transparent and put all of your cards on the table, you are in the best place to change and grow, whether personally or within a relationship (providing the other person embraces your vision and expectation for transformation).

Two individuals who are open and honest with each other can spur one another on in their sanctification (Hebrews 10:25). Discipleship happens this way. And from that excellent starting point, it is a matter of ongoing communication.

Let's say my fictional characters, Mark and Mandy, are being practically animated by the gospel. They have nothing to hide and nothing to fear. They are for each other and want to be a means of grace in each other's lives. If that is where they are, here are some excellent questions that will radicalize their lives and marriage.

You're welcome to put your Bible down, walk out of your prayer closet, and engage your closest relationships with these questions too. Pick one and start talking:

1. What is God doing in your life? How are you succeeding, and how are you struggling?

2. What are some things I am doing that are helping you mature in Christ? How do I hinder you in your walk with the Lord?

3. What are some of your fears? What do those fears tempt you to do?

4. What is an ongoing struggle you have in your life? When did it begin? What have you been doing about it? How can I help you?

5. What is something you would like to control, but you cannot control, and you struggle with it?

6. In your opinion, how does God see you? I am not asking for a biblical answer but your answer.

7. In your opinion, how do others see you? Are there certain people with whom you struggle? Why do you struggle? What do you think the Lord wants to teach you? How can I help you with this?

8. What regrets do you have? What about guilt or shame related things?

9. What hinders our relationship, and how could I change to make it better?

10. What is something that I am not asking, but you think it would be helpful for me to ask?

Now put this book down and become a practical, active doer of God's Word.

Chapter 34

It Is Finished

Congratulations!

You have finished the book. Now it is time to get started if you haven't already. Throughout this book, I have asked you some hard questions. Have you been answering them along the way?

If you haven't, I appeal to you to pick out a chapter that you would like to work on and let the questions penetrate your heart as you ask the Lord to help you change. Also, it would be best to meet with a friend and work through the chapter together.

This book is not meant to be placed on a shelf and replaced by another. It could take you years to master its content. You have finished the book, but the Lord is not finished with you. If I can serve you, please let me know. I'll be in my cyber home. It would be a joy to come alongside you as you continue working out what the Lord is working into you.

God bless,

Rick

About the Author

Rick Thomas has been training in the Upstate of South Carolina since 1997. After several years as a counselor and pastor, he founded and launched his training organization to encourage and equip people for effective living.

In the early '90s, he earned a BA in Theology. Later he received a BS in Education. Rick became ordained into Christian ministry in 1993, and in 2000, he graduated with an MA in Counseling. The Association of Certified Biblical Counselors recognized him as a Fellow in 2006.

Today his organization reaches people in every country through training, blogging, podcasting, counseling, and coaching. His cyber home is RickThomas.Net.

Join Our Team

Our community is a gathering of individuals from all over the world who are seeking to live more productive and inspiring lives. We all have situational and relational challenges that could benefit from having other people bringing insight and care.

Caring for others is what our community does best.

Community Resources

- Access to a stocked library of content written from a God-centered, others-centered perspective
- Live and archived webinars
- Training presentations, videos, infographics, mind maps, best practices, and more
- Private membership-only forum for questions and answers about life and relationships

- Opportunities to ask Rick and his team key questions that are important to you
- A 24/7 all-access "life coach" for personal development and training of others
- A self-paced Mastermind Training Program: Distance Education

Partner with Us

We are a membership-supported community. You can also partner with us by making a one-time or recurring donation. We are a 501(c) 3 NPO. Go to our ministry website, RickThomas.Net, to learn more.

Printed in Great Britain
by Amazon